DRED SCOTT
v.
SANDFORD

The Pursuit of Freedom

GREAT SUPREME COURT DECISIONS

Brown v. Board of Education
Dred Scott v. Sandford
Engel v. Vitale
Marbury v. Madison
Miranda v. Arizona
Plessy v. Ferguson
Regents of the University of California v. Bakke
Roe v. Wade

Great Supreme Court Decisions

31271

DRED SCOTT
━ V. ━
SANDFORD

The Pursuit of Freedom

Tim McNeese

CHELSEA HOUSE
PUBLISHERS
An imprint of Infobase Publishing

Dred Scott v. Sandford

Chelsea House
An imprint of Infobase Publishing
132 West 31st Street
New York NY 10001

Library of Congress Cataloging-in-Publication Data
McNeese, Tim.
Dred Scott v. Sandford / Tim McNeese.
        p. cm. — (Great Supreme Court decisions)
Includes bibliographical references and index.
ISBN 0-7910-9236-4 (hardcover)
1. Scott, Dred, 1809–1858—Trials, litigation, etc.—Juvenile literature.
2. Sanford, John F. A., 1806 or 7–1857—Trials, litigation, etc.—Juvenile literature. 3. Slavery—Law and legislation—United States—History—Juvenile literature. 4. Slavery—United States—Legal status of slaves in free states—Juvenile literature.
I. Title: Dred Scott versus Sandford. II. Title. III. Series.
  KF228.S27M36 2006
  342.7308'7—dc22   2006007326

Series design by Erika K. Arroyo
Cover design by Takeshi Takahashi

Printed in the United States of America

Bang CHP 10 9 8 7 6 5 4 3 2 1

This book is printed on acid-free paper.

All links and Web addresses were checked and verified to be correct at the time of publication. Because of the dynamic nature of the Web, some addresses and links may have changed since publication and may no longer be valid.

EQUAL·JUSTICE·UNDER·LAW·

Contents

Introduction

Across the nation's capital, Washington City, the sky was clear and the air cool and crisp. The city was buzzing with anxious talk and anticipation. It had already been an exciting week. Two days earlier, a new American president had been sworn in, the nation's fifteenth chief executive, a Pennsylvania Democrat and a bachelor named James Buchanan. No one was certain how Buchanan would handle the ongoing and widening rift between those who supported the expansion of the institution of slavery into the western territories and those who wanted the system of black servitude to remain where it was—in the South. Would he, as a Northerner, take a solid stand against slavery moving farther west? Would he, as a Democrat who needed political support from his fellow party members in the South, allow for their "peculiar institution," as southerners referred to slavery, to move beyond the Mississippi River into the northern reaches of the vast

Nebraska Territory? It was the question that had divided Americans north and south since the founding of the great American republic 70 years earlier. In America's future, where would slavery exist? To where would it be allowed to expand? Where the answers to these questions—with all their potential for regional animosities—might take the nation, no one knew.

Although the inauguration was over, new political excitement was sweeping across the city, as well as the nation. The attention of many that spring morning was focused on events scheduled to take place on the hill, inside the Capitol building. It was there that both houses of the United States Congress met, where its representatives and senators discussed proposed legislation; engaged in lengthy, sometimes heated debates; then cast their votes, creating laws for the ever-expanding American republic. On this day, March 6, 1857, though, Congress was adjourned, having ended its spring session just three days earlier. Instead, another branch of the federal government was meeting on the hill—the nine justices of the United States Supreme Court.

Dred Scott was a slave whose fight for freedom would go all the way to the U.S. Supreme Court. The court's decision would affect him and all black people living in the United States.

The members of the highest court in the nation met in a dimly lit, ground level courtroom situated deep within the Capitol building. Above the courtroom was the small Senate chamber. One newspaper reporter wrote that the courtroom resembled "a potato hole of a place . . . a queer room of small dimensions and shaped overhead like a quarter section of a pumpkin shell."[1] On a normal day, when the court met, few people attended its sessions. Capitol Hill drama was usually found on the Senate floor or in the House chamber, where fiery debates would sometimes explode between skilled orators. Today, however, the court chamber was packed with news reporters and a gallery of spectators. Throughout the courtroom, the audience that had gathered awaited the justices and their decision regarding the fate of one individual, a slave named Dred Scott. As the Supreme Court justices prepared to announce their opinion, all parties—jurists, journalists, audience, and American citizens—knew their words concerning the fate of this single slave litigant would ripple across the country and determine slavery's future.

At 11:00 A.M., the nine justices, each wearing traditional black robes, stepped into view of the gathered crowd. An expectant buzz filled the gallery. At the head of the robed line walked the elderly Chief Justice, Roger B. Taney, who would turn 80 years old in less than two weeks. Although Taney was a tall man, he walked with a stoop, bent with age. He appeared ill, although some believed he was simply a hypochondriac who fretted constantly about his health. In his hands he held a brief, the ruling he would soon read to the assembled crowd—a ruling that would lay down a decision in a case that had been already through three lower courts over the past 11 years, a case now bearing the title *Dred Scott v. Sandford.*

Ironically, perhaps, neither litigant—Scott nor Sanford (the name was misspelled by a court clerk)—were present in the courtroom that morning. As for Scott, he was back in St. Louis, Missouri, still working as a slave. For him, the day was like any other. As for his owner, John Sanford, the man Scott was suing for his freedom, as well as the freedom of his wife, Harriet, and their two daughters, Eliza and Lizzie, his absence from the courtroom was unavoidable. Sanford was locked up in an insane asylum. In just a few weeks, he would die there, never knowing the results of the decision concerning the freedom of the Scott family.

Scott's suit against his master claimed that because he had been taken north from a slave state to free states and territories, where slavery did not exist, he should be granted his freedom. Originally, he filed suit in Missouri. There, in 1850, a lower court decided in Scott's favor and ordered the Missouri-held slave freed. Two years later, however, the Missouri Supreme Court ruled against Scott. Having appealed his case to the highest court in the land, Scott and his family were possibly now in unsympathetic hands. For those who knew the makeup of the Supreme Court and the backgrounds of the nine justices, the future of the Scotts did not look promising. Chief Justice Taney, a wealthy southerner, had always been a supporter of slavery. He had even engaged in buying and selling slaves as a young man. Four additional justices were also proslavery southerners. Two more were northerners known as "doughfaces," who supported slavery. Only one justice among the nine on the court had ever declared himself an opponent of slavery.

Even as the court met to hand down its momentous decision that spring day in 1857, considerable time had passed since the case was first presented to the justices. The lawyer handling Scott's case was a Washington City attorney originally from St. Louis, where Scott and his family lived. His name was Montgomery Blair. In earlier years, he had served as mayor of St. Louis, but in 1852, he moved to Washington to practice law. He was the perfect man to represent Scott's case before the Supreme Court. He understood both sides in the case and was keenly aware of how southerners thought about their institution of slavery. In addition, Blair had first argued the Scott case more than a year earlier, in February 1856.

In the months that followed the lawyers' presentations of the case, the justices on the Supreme Court did not turn around an

A PUBLIC MEETING

WILL BE HELD ON

THURSDAY EVENING, 2D INSTANT,

at 7; o'clock, in ISRAEL CHURCH, to consider the atrocious decision of the Supreme Court in the

DRED SCOTT CASE,

and other outrages to which the colored people are subject under the Constitution of the United States.

C. L. REMOND,

ROBERT PURVIS,

and others will be speakers on the occasion. Mrs. MOTT, Mr. M'KIM and B. S. JONES of Ohio, have also accepted invitations to be present. All persons are invited to attend. Admittance free.

The Dred Scott lawsuit stirred up emotions all over the United States; it seemed many people had a stake in the case's outcome. This 1857 poster advertises a church meeting to discuss the "atrocious decision."

immediate decision. Then, the justices had called Blair and Sanford's lawyers back to make more arguments before the court. In December 1856, lawyers for both Scott and Sanford finally concluded presenting their arguments in the Supreme Court chamber. Now, three months later, the justices were ready to give an answer to Scott, Sanford, and the nation: Would Scott and his family be free? Would slavery be allowed to expand into free territories? Could slavery still be restricted in states that had banned the institution from their borders?

As the justices took their seats, the room fell quiet. Reporters readied their pencils and notepads. The audience sat silently, anxiously waiting to hear their majority decision. Taney took his seat and began reading from the papers in front of him. For the next two hours, he read aloud, his aged hands feeble and shaking. As Taney spoke, his words trailed off as his voice increasingly weakened. When he finished, other justices took their turns, making their positions clear, both in support of Scott and in opposition. These presentations stretched through the entire day and into the next. When their voices finally fell silent, however, the future of Dred Scott, his family, and the immediate status of slavery and its potential to expand into new American territory was clear. The decision would be as controversial as the circumstances that helped to create the case in the first place. It further divided the country along regional lines, North and South. The decision would become, in the words of Abraham Lincoln, "an astonisher in legal history."[2]

The Origins
of American
Slavery

1

After a generation of failed attempts, Britain planted its first successful colonial foothold along the Atlantic Coast of North America early in the seventeenth century. This adventurous group set out from England late in 1606 and reached the Tidewater region of Chesapeake Bay the following May. That spring, three small boatloads of 140 men and 4 boys established a settlement fort along the banks of the James River in Virginia. (They named the river for their king, James I, and Virginia after Queen Elizabeth I, whose subjects referred to her as the "Virgin Queen.") Over the next 12 years, the Jamestown settlers struggled to keep their colony alive. Many died from disease, Indian attack, and starvation.

This lithograph depicts the arrival of African slaves to the colony of Jamestown, Virginia, in 1619. The slaves were considered cargo but were initially treated the same as the colony's white indentured servants.

Slowly, the colonists adapted to their New World surroundings and created a unique world for themselves. To provide a much needed economic base for the colony, they began planting Caribbean tobacco as a cash crop. Women soon arrived at the colony to marry the men and raise families. By 1619, two additionally significant changes took place. The Jamestown colonists chose representatives to the first elected legislature in America, the House of Burgesses. A new group of residents was also introduced to Jamestown that year. They were black workers delivered to the English colonial settlement aboard a Dutch ship, *Jesus of Lubeck*. According to John Rolfe, one of Jamestown's leading citizens, "About the last of August came a dutch man of warre that sold us twenty Negars."[3] These arrivals would be the first African blacks in English North America. In that same year, then, the seeds of both representative government and African slavery were sown in the English colonies.

CREATING AMERICAN SLAVERY

Slavery was not introduced immediately with the arrival of a handful of Africans on Virginia soil. With plenty of available poor, white workers—those who worked temporarily as indentured servants to pay off their ship's passage to America—the number of blacks imported into the English colonies of North America remained small. Even as late as 1649, only 300 blacks had arrived in Virginia. In addition, for decades following the arrival of those first Africans at Jamestown, blacks were treated as servants, not slaves bound to work for their masters for life.

Then, things changed. White English colonists began to treat black workers differently. By 1650, these servants were being described as slaves. Laws were created in support of this shift in the status of Africans in the English colonies. A system of institutionalized slavery developed, binding black workers to a life as property, laboring endlessly. What caused this shift by Virginia landowners and plantation proprietors away from their earlier reliance on white indentured servants, only to replace them with a labor force based on black slavery? Several reasons are clear. Until about 1650, it cost landowners less to pay the passage of a poor English immigrant to the Atlantic colonies than to purchase a slave. During these years, too, there was a high death rate among both white and black workers, whether indentured or black servants. About half of immigrant workers died within their first five years in America. With a slave costing twice as much as a white indentured servant, it was economically less profitable and did not make good business sense to purchase a black worker instead of indenturing a white servant. The best deal for the landowner was in an indenture. In addition, there were plenty of indentured servants available to work in the North American colonies through the first half of the seventeenth century. By the 1650s and 1660s, however, the number of available indentured servants began to drop. In England, by that time, working conditions for the poor were improving, and other advantages were coming to these would-be immigrants. So, fewer left England for America. The available number of white indentured servants in colonial America was dwindling, but colonial landowners still needed a viable work force, so they turned to black workers.

In 1662, the Virginia House of Burgesses put its stamp of approval on the developing system of slavery by passing a law stating that the children of slave mothers inherited the status of their mothers. This meant they would be born slaves. By 1671, an additional Virginia law significantly reduced the punishment handed out to slave masters who "accidentally" killed their slaves while punishing them. Within two generations of the arrival of the *Jesus of Lubeck* in Jamestown, slavery had been defined and classified by law in America. Other colonies would follow Virginia's lead. New York institutionalized lifelong slavery for Africans brought to its colony in 1665. In 1671, the Maryland legislature began passing laws establishing slavery in that colony. In time, all the British colonies along the Atlantic Coast had created a system of black slavery.

The institution would be fine-tuned, with additional laws passed during the remainder of the century and the beginning of the next. By 1705, the slave laws of Virginia had been written to address nearly every aspect of slave life. The entire package of relevant slave laws was called the Virginia Negro Code. Some of these laws seem especially cruel, such as the following, from Virginia (1699):

> For the first offence of hog stealing commited by a Negro or slave he shall be carried before a justice of the peace of the county where the fact was commited before whome being convicted of the said offence by one evidence or by his owne confession he shall . . . receive on his bare back thirty nine lashes well laid on, and for the second offence such Negro or slave upon conviction before a court of record shall stand two hours in the pillory and have both his eares nailed thereto and at the expiration of the said two hours have his ears cutt off close by the nailes.[4]

Such laws restricted the lives of Virginia's slaves by controlling their freedom of movement and reducing or eliminating their civil rights. According to these laws, a slave could not testify in court as a witness against a white person. He or she could not own personal property. Slaves could not own guns and did not have the right to assemble freely. When traveling outside his master's property, a slave had to carry a special pass. Even marriages between slaves were not recognized as valid and binding by Virginia law. All such laws caused black slaves to be regarded as little more than property. They became objects of prejudice and condescension:

> At law, a slave was reduced in considerable degree from a person to a thing, having no legitimate will of its own and belonging bodily to its owner. As property, a slave could

be bought and sold. As animate property, he could be compelled to work, and his offspring belonged absolutely to the master. Thus a slave was in some respects like a domestic animal, being an item of wealth, virtually a beast of burden, and a creature requiring constant supervision and restraint.[5]

One historian described the process of creating slavery in the colonies as follows, "In short, first came the Negro, then the institution of slavery, and finally racism of the kind that asserts the genetic inferiority of the Negro."[6]

THE SPREAD OF SLAVERY

Once slavery was defined as an American institution, its roots ran deep. With the number of white indentured servants in decline by the late 1600s and early 1700s, the English colonies along the Atlantic Coast were threatened with a shortage of workers. The easy answer appeared to be to import even more Africans.

With slavery institutionalized in all the British colonies, and an increasing need for workers, the number of blacks delivered along the Atlantic Coast rose considerably. In 1680, in Maryland, white servants outnumbered slaves by a ratio of four to one. Twenty years later, black workers outnumbered white indentured servants. By 1710, slaves outnumbered white workers five to one. In the southern colonies, where black laborers were used to raise vast crops of tobacco, rice, and indigo, the percentage of black workers was much higher than that of the northern colonies—33 percent of workers were black. In Virginia, one out of every five persons was black. In South Carolina, the percentage was double that number.

In fact, even though slavery existed in all of the English colonies along the Atlantic Coast, most of the slaves were held in the southern colonies. By the time of the American Revolution (1775–1783), slaves made up 40 percent of the non–

Native American population of the southern colonies. There were more differences between the slave populations of the South and the other colonial regions than just simply numbers, however. Even though the system of slavery and its required laws of control were pretty much the same from Massachusetts in the North to Georgia in the South, "the daily life of a New England house servant bore little resemblance to the life of a field hand on a South Carolina rice plantation."[7] It would be southern slavery that would typify the institution of American slavery. Across the South, slaves worked as agriculturalists. Two Southern slave regions developed by the early 1700s. Slaves worked the tobacco fields of the Tidewater region, which included Maryland and Virginia, and in the Lower South—North and South Carolina and Georgia—they raised and harvested rice.

While working in close proximity with one another on southern farms and plantations, especially on larger plantations where dozens or even hundreds lived and worked side by side, black slaves developed their own cultures. These slave cultures varied from place to place and region to region, but they often comprised elements of both life in America and African social and cultural practices. Slaves kept African religious ideas and superstitions, even as they lost their traditional languages (because slaves in the British colonies were expected to speak English).

Black Africans brought their customary fashions and traditional musical instruments, including the *mbanza*, a plucked stringed instrument fashioned from a gourd that became the forerunner of the American banjo. They also brought to their New World homes different ways of singing, including antiphonal, or the "call-and-response" style of, singing. Forced to create family structures despite legal restrictions and the constant possibility that a spouse or family member might be sold off, never to be seen again, slaves created their own ways of getting married and raising children. By the mid-1700s, slaves had developed a highly structured system of cultures, all of them designed to help the slaves cope and survive the difficulties and restrictions of institutionalized slavery.

By 1750, then, slavery was well entrenched and a significant aspect of the economic system found in the British colonies along the Atlantic Coast. Slaves provided the major labor force from the Tidewater to Georgia. Slavery existed in the northern colonies, but it was much less important there. Of the entire slave population found in the British colonies of North America at mid-eighteenth century, only one in ten slaves lived outside the South. In South Carolina, blacks outnumbered whites. Overall, slaves constituted 25 percent of the non–Native American population in the southern colonies. By the time of the American Revolution, just one generation later, the black slave population in the South had risen to

A group of slaves sings on a plantation, in this woodcut from the 1850s. Although they were taken from their homes and stripped of their basic freedoms, African slaves maintained their customs as best they could in the United States. Language, music, holidays, and family structure were important traditions to hold on to.

approximately 40 percent of the total. It appeared that black slavery in the South was there to stay.

By comparison, the northern slave population was almost inconsequential. Of an estimated total slave population in the 13 colonies of 700,000, only 40,000 were held outside the South. The Middle Colonies—New York, Pennsylvania, New Jersey, and Delaware—had a slave population of about 36,000, whereas New England only claimed 4,000. Also, slave populations of the South were growing and were not dependent on continued slave importation to keep their numbers up. Without question, slaves were imported into the British colonies during every decade of the 1700s. Between 1700 and 1770, about 80,000 were imported into the Tidewater colonies of Virginia and Maryland alone.

An even larger number of slaves developed through slave parents having children, however. This phenomenon of "natural increase" was unique to the British colonies. Nowhere else in the Western Hemisphere where slavery existed did the slave population rise simply by slaves producing children. This was largely because in the British North American colonies, slaves were generally never considered as expendable (replaceable). In other places, such as the Caribbean or South American Brazil, where the profits from slave-produced sugar were enormous, slave populations could regularly be worked to death and replaced every four or five years. Because tobacco was the only significant cash crop in the North American colonies (and even then, its profit margin was nowhere close to that of the lucrative sugar market), owners hoped to keep their slaves alive and productive as long as possible. These economic circumstances brought about two significant circumstances regarding British North American slavery: (1) Only about 5 percent of the slaves brought from Africa to the New World between 1500 and the 1800 were delivered in the British colonies along the Atlantic Coast, and (2) American slaves had greater opportunities to create well-defined, multigenerational family units.

THE AMERICAN REVOLUTION

From the years of its establishment in the seventeenth century, and well into the eighteenth century, slavery developed in the British colonies without significant controversy and through a haphazard, unplanned series of events. The practice was so common in America that, as one historian has written, "Slavery remained a largely unexamined fact of life."[8] By the final decades of the eighteenth century, institutionalized slavery had existed for more than a century in the British colonies hugging the Atlantic Coast. Before that, blacks had worked in the colonies by another half century. Slavery was a foregone conclusion as a major aspect of economic life in America.

In the 1760s and 1770s, however, opportunities arose in the colonies that gave those morally opposed to slavery some hope that it might one day cease to exist. During those decades, British colonials began questioning their continued relationship with Great Britain as obedient subjects of the Crown. By 1775, the colonies were in open rebellion, and the American Revolutionary War—a conflict between British authorities and patriot Americans that would result in the colonies gaining their independence from Britain—was under way. Throughout the conflict, such ideals as freedom and liberty were constantly on the mind of every American revolutionary patriot and supporter. As rebellious Americans began talking about liberty, they began to view the institution of slavery through a new lens. It appeared to some patriots that talking of liberty while holding men and women as slaves did not make much sense and even seemed hypocritical. As one patriot leader and essayist, James Otis from Massachusetts, stated, "The Colonists are by law of Nature free born as indeed all men are, white or black. . . . Does it follow that 'tis right to enslave a man because he is black?"[9] Other patriot voices agreed. Thomas Paine wrote revolutionary pamphlets that provided ideological support for many patriots on behalf of the ideal of independence. In his 1776 pamphlet *Common Sense*, which was read by tens of thousands of supporters of the revolution, he noted how some patriots "complain so loudly of attempts to enslave them," while those same sons of liberty "hold so many hundred thousands in slavery; and annually enslave many thousands more."[10] But, even as Thomas Jefferson of Virginia wrote his *Declaration of Independence* that "all men are created equal," he did not intend to apply the maxim to slaves or even to black people as a whole. Jefferson himself was a slave owner, as was George Washington, the commander-in-chief of the patriot army.

Even though about 5,000 blacks fought on the American side during the Revolutionary War (many in hopes that they would receive their freedom in exchange for fighting for "liberty"), they emerged from the war with slavery still practiced across the South. The institution was dealt a mortal blow in the North, however. By 1784, every northern state except two—New Jersey and New York—had passed legislation designed to eliminate slavery in these states immediately or to end the institution within a certain period of time. In some southern states, however, especially Virginia, the House of Burgesses passed a law requiring that all slaves within the commonwealth who fought for the American cause during the Revolutionary War be freed. Elsewhere in the South, the Revolutionary War caused some slave masters to free their slaves. These included a plantation owner named Philip Graham, who wrote that "fellow men in bondage and slavery is repugnant to the gold law of god and the unalienable right of mankind as well as to every principle of the late glorious revolution which has taken place in America."[11] Despite similar antislavery attitudes scattered throughout the South, and the American Revolutionary War, slavery continued, although it emerged from the Revolution a changed institution.

Another event came very close to eliminating slavery, however. Following the war, a drop in the price of tobacco caused production to be cut back dramatically. The British market, after all, was no longer interested in buying American tobacco. As plantation owners and southern farmers scrambled to shift production to grains and away from tobacco, the need for hundreds of thousands of slaves was significantly reduced. With grain production requiring less field labor, some slave owners began to free their slaves after a specified number of years of service. As a

THE U.S. CONSTITUTION AND SLAVERY

In the years just following the successful end to the American Revolution, an end that brought America's independence from Great Britain, the situation of slavery in the former colonies appeared to be in transition. The issue was so divisive that it would prove to be one of the most serious challenges to keeping the new nation of the United States together after the Revolution.

At the Constitutional Convention of 1787, discussion of slavery did not focus on whether or not the institution should continue. The real issue was representation. The argument had to do with how or whether slaves could be counted in establishing a state's representational proportion. As decided at the Convention, a state's representation would be based, in part, on how many people lived in that state. It was not an issue in creating the Senate. Each state, whether they had a large or small population, would be able to appoint two senators. But membership in the other body of Congress, the House of Representatives, was based on the actual number of residents in the state. The larger the state's population, the larger its number of elected representatives in the House. Because the southern states were home to hundreds of thousands of slaves, those states wanted their slaves to count for representation. Northerners found that unacceptable. Those slaves, northerners argued, were not able to vote, would not be truly represented because they had few recognizable rights by law, and should not be counted the same as free men. Slaves, northerners stated, should not be considered as people when a state's population was counted for representation. They must be considered strictly as property.

result, thousands of slaves were freed. To some observers, during the final decade of the 1700s, it appeared that slavery was a dying American institution.

The issue over slavery and how to count black workers for representation had already been answered several years earlier during debates over the Articles of Confederation. In 1783, designers of the Articles had compromised on the issue and decided to count slaves as a fraction, with each slave counted as three-fifths of a person for purposes of representation and taxation. The fraction had been agreed on, but it had not been put into practice. Faced again with the same relative dilemma, the delegates at the 1787 Constitutional Convention reached an acceptable compromise on the issue. They simply invoked the three-fifths rule. The rule might have quieted for a time arguments between northerners and southerners, but it did not sit well with everyone, including some southerners. One such southerner was James Madison, from Virginia. Although he was a slave owner who supported the three-fifths rule, he believed it "wrong to admit in the Constitution the idea that there could be property in men."*

During the years that followed, however, the three-fifths compromise appeared to favor the southern states. Counting slaves for taxation purposes proved insignificant and unimportant. By being able to count slaves for representation, Southern states were able to hold about 30 percent more of the seats in the House than they would have been able to if their slaves had not been counted, even as a fraction.

* Quoted in Don E. Fehrenbacher, *The Dred Scott Case: Its Significance in American Law & Politics*. New York: Oxford University Press, 1978, p. 21.

For the moment, although almost no one suggested that slavery be purposefully eliminated throughout the South, Southerners and Northerners joined together in support of limiting the future expansion of slavery. During the summer months of 1787, America's new political leaders met in Philadelphia to hammer out a national constitution. Within that document, one that created a federal system of government for the new United States, the delegates at the convention agreed to establish a date for stopping the importation of new slaves into the former British colonies. The year to end the international slave trade was set at 1808.

Even earlier, between the end of the American Revolution (1783) and the writing of the U.S. Constitution (1787), the fledging postrevolutionary government issued a law creating the Northwest Territory, which today includes the states of Ohio, Indiana, Illinois, Michigan, and Wisconsin. Under the Northwest Ordinance of 1787, this new region was established without slavery.

There were other signs that slavery was in decline. By the end of the 1780s, state laws allowing owners to voluntarily free their slaves were passed. These laws also allowed slaves to buy their own freedom. Such laws were written and passed in Virginia (1782), Delaware (1787), Maryland (1790), and the newly added western state of Kentucky (1792). By the 1790s, all states north of Virginia had abolition societies—groups devoted to bringing about the end of slavery in America. Several of the nation's founding fathers, who had helped fight the American Revolutionary War and create the U.S. Constitution in 1787 (including Benjamin Franklin, Alexander Hamilton, and the first Supreme Court Chief Justice, John Jay), played important roles in these early abolition movements. As America approached the final years of the eighteenth century, the winds of change appeared to be blowing against the continuation of slavery in the new United States.

EQUAL·JUSTICE·UNDER·LAW

2

A New Era of Slavery

Once the new United States Constitution became the law of the land, the institution of slavery was guaranteed protection by federal law. This did not mean that states could not keep the institution from their borders, however. Slavery had always existed through "local common and statute law in the thirteen colonies."[12] Under the Constitution of 1787 (which is basically the same constitution in place in the United States today), slavery continued to exist under local and state laws. In some ways, it was similar to other institutions found in the states (for example, marriage, private land ownership, and inheritance laws) that were regulated on the state level. There was one important difference, however. States had the power not only to protect and regulate slavery; they also had the power to ban its existence within their borders. The bottom line was always clear: At any time, in any state, slavery could be banned.

Consequently, by the 1790s, many considered the end of slavery to be near at hand. Tobacco production was no longer as profitable as it had been before the Revolutionary War. Rice production also dropped off, and indigo, another slave labor–produced southern crop, was dying out as an important commodity. As American farming began shifting increasingly toward wheat and corn production—crops that did not require nine months of involved labor, as did tobacco—the southern economy no longer required large numbers of slaves to work in fields over long, endless days. Slavery no longer paid, it seemed to many. Unless the South developed a different cash crop, slavery's end seemed to actually be within reach.

THE COTTON GIN AND FUGITIVE SLAVES

By the 1790s, the future of slavery in the young United States lay in doubt. Then, in 1793, another event, at first seemingly unrelated to the future of slavery in the United States, changed everything. That year, a northern mechanic and tinkerer named Eli Whitney invented a mechanical device that would change the nature of southern agriculture and the future of slavery. His hand-cranked device was called the cotton gin (the word gin being short for "engine"). This simple machine would prove to be one of the most important in American history.

Prior to Whitney's invention of this simple device, cotton production in America, including the South, was inconsequential. Although the bushy fiber crop grew well in the South, which had a long growing season, good soil, and hot temperatures, cotton production was difficult. Slave labor could be utilized to provide the long hours of "stoop labor" required in cotton fields (mostly hoeing the weeds away from the cotton plants, which were susceptible to weed infestation), but the real problem was

African slaves use the first cotton gin, in this woodcut from 1869. The invention of the cotton gin created a need for more slave labor in the South.

in "cleaning" the cotton bolls once they were picked in the field. Short staple cotton, the kind that could be grown easily across the South, produced cotton that was loaded with small, green, sticky seeds—the "short staples." Cleaning the seeds out of the cotton bolls was a slow process. One field slave could pick 50 pounds of cotton in a day, but it would take a single worker a month to clean that amount of cotton. This problem produced a costly bottleneck in American cotton production. That is, until Whitney invented his cotton engine. This simple device featured matching rollers sporting rows of teeth that passed one another when the gin's crank was turned. These teeth would pull the cotton lint through, while leaving the thicker seeds behind, dropping them into a box below the rollers. According to Whitney, "I made a [model] . . . which required the labour of one man to turn it and with which one man will clean ten times as much cotton as he can in any other way before known and also clean it much better than the usual mode."[13] This simple machine, one that could easily fit on a table top, revolutionized cotton production and raised a new call for the continuation of slavery in America. The South had found its new cash crop, causing slavery and cotton to become linked in American history.

That same year boasted another significant mile marker concerning American slavery. With the northern states either banning slavery immediately or creating processes for its gradual elimination, southern slaves looked to the North as a place of refuge. When slavery existed in all 13 colonies, there was no place to which an escaped slave could safely run and remain in the colonies; but as this situation changed, slave owners began to demand that the federal government protect their slaves. When Congress met in 1789, the issue of slaves escaping into the North was barely mentioned. By 1793, during the

This lithograph delivers a sharp message against the Fugitive Slave Act passed by Congress in September 1850. The artwork features a gang of white men hunting down and shooting a group of black men (whether they are freed or escaped is unclear).

second session of Congress, however, the call for protective action was issued. The result was the passage of the Fugitive Slave Law of 1793.

The law was worded vaguely, but it stipulated that when a person "held to service or labor" escaped from a slave state into a free state (a state where slavery did not legally exist) that, if his or her owner laid claim to the runaway black worker, the escaped slave must be "delivered up" and returned back to his or her owner to serve as a slave once again.[14] This new law, then, would allow a slave owner or someone designated to represent him to cross over into a free state (or another slave state) and recapture the fugitive slave. Then, under the law, the owner was to take his recaptured slave before a judge—it did not matter whether he was a federal, state, or even local judge—and there show "proof" that he owned the escaped slave. He would then be given a certificate authorizing the owner to return to his farm or plantation with his runaway slave. Anyone interfering with the recapture of an escaped slave, even in a free territory or state, was subject to heavy fines. The proposed Fugitive Slave Bill was unopposed in the Senate and was passed in the House by a vote of 48 to 7. Perhaps ironically, this newly devised law regarding the recapture of fugitive slaves was not created because slaves were escaping in serious numbers over state lines into free states. It was the South's way of looking ahead toward an uncertain future, when its slaves might take advantage of the North's increasing moves away from slavery, including banning the institution.

Although the law passed overwhelmingly, it created much controversy, especially in the arena of power splitting between the federal government and the various state governments. In creating the Fugitive Slave Law of 1793, "Congress voted to invade state sovereignty for the benefit of the slaveholder, issuing him a kind of vigilante's license to enforce his rights himself with a minimum of formality."[15] The law bypassed what were otherwise standard legal processes, including a trial by jury. Requirements of evidence were extremely limited, and a slave holder's claim of ownership was considered proof enough. Also, the alleged escaped slave had no right to testify on his or her behalf in court and was not protected from self-incrimination. To make matters worse, there was no time limit written into the act. A slave owner could make a claim against a black person living in the free North many years after his or her alleged escape. All in all, the Fugitive Slave Law of 1793 offered no protections or guarantees on behalf of those accused of being escaped slaves. For a slave, escaping into a free, northern state was no guarantee that he or she would not be recaptured and returned to slavery once again. The law would remain in effect for nearly 60 years, until it was replaced in 1850 by an even more severe law.

The Fugitive Slave Law of 1793 addressed what should happen if a southern slave escaped from his master and then came into a northern state for refuge. What if a master took a slave into a free state or territory by choice, though? Despite the federal law, questions lingered for decades over whether slaves could be taken into free states and territories by their masters and still remain slaves. The question was a thorny one:

> What happened to the legal condition of a slave entering a no slaveholding jurisdiction? And if he later returned to a slaveholding state, what counter-effect did that return have upon whatever change of condition had been wrought by his stay in the free state or territory? By the early decades of the nineteenth century, this problem of the status of slaves residing or once resident on free soil had already become one of the classic issues in the legal history of slavery.[16]

There were three answers to the question, although there was little agreement as to which one was most acceptable. One theory suggested that a slave remained a slave even when he entered a free state. This was, after all, the point of the 1793 Fugitive Slave Law, but there had to be limits in the law's interpretaton; otherwise, slavery was always protected everywhere by federal law regardless of the wishes of a specific state concerning slavery. A second theory was that a slave taken into a free state by his master (not an escaped slave) became a free individual, since slavery did not exist legally in that free state and that the slave in question remained free permanently. This principle—often called "once free, forever free"—limited the Fugitive Slave Law only to escaped slaves, not those freely taken by a master into a free state or territory. The third theory stated that a slave taken by his master into a free state or territory was free until he was taken back into a state where slavery existed. At that point, the temporarily freed black was a slave once again.

Further complicating these three theories was the question of how much time a slave had spent in a free state. The question was a crucial one. Various legal minds, as well as existing laws, made a distinction between a master taking a slave into a free state only for travel or to "sojourn" into that state and remaining there long enough for the slave owner's presence to constitute permanent residence or "domicile." The distinction between "sojourn" and "domicile" was not easily defined and could be extremely subtle, but important, in determining a lack of caution on the part of a slave owner in bringing his slave into a free state. (Ironically, perhaps, southern courts typically upheld the principle of "once free, forever free" when cases surrounding this issue arose during the late eighteenth and early nineteenth centuries.) The American legal system wrestled and redefined its views on this issue repeatedly until the Dred Scott case was decided in the 1850s.

SLAVERY'S EXPANSION AND THE MISSOURI COMPROMISE

During those same decades, slavery experienced a revival in its economic importance and in the number of slaves living in the United States and its territories. As the number of slaves in the South increased significantly during the first two decades of the 1800s, the number of slave states and territories also increased.

Prior to 1820, five new slave states were added to the young United States. These included Kentucky, Tennessee, Louisiana, Mississippi, and Alabama. Slavery spread across the South from the Atlantic Coast south of Chesapeake Bay clear to the Mississippi River. With the admission of Louisiana as a slave state, the institution of perpetual bondage was extended even west of the Mississippi and into the Louisiana Purchase Territory, the western region acquired by President Thomas Jefferson from the French in 1803. (The territory was vast, stretching north to the Canadian border, with the Mississippi River providing its eastern border and its western line marked by the Rocky Mountains of the far West.) By 1819, the number of slave states and free states was evenly balanced at 11 each. This meant that, in the Senate, with each state allowed two senators, there was an equilibrium between slave and free states.

But that year, the balance between the slave-holding states and the free was threatened. Another western territory, Missouri, had made application for statehood two years earlier, in 1817. The application called for Missouri to be admitted as a slave state. Because the vast Louisiana Territory was being made into a slave state, Northerners feared that slavery might eventually extend throughout the region, resulting in the number of slave states vastly outnumbering free ones. Northern politicians dug in their heels, intent on halting the advance of slavery outside the Deep South. Debate continued on Missouri's application until 1819. Just as the Senate was preparing to vote on statehood for Missouri, a New York senator, James Tallmadge, proposed an amendment, one that would deny any additional slaves to be brought into Missouri. In addition, all slaves already in Missouri would be freed when they reached 25 years of age. The move immediately raised the ire of Southerners everywhere. One southern politician, Thomas Ritchie, warned his fellow slave supporters: "If we yield now, beware. [The North] will ride us forever."[17] The amended application passed in the House, but the Senate rejected it just before Congress adjourned its session.

The issue of Missouri's statehood was splitting the Congress. At the center of the ongoing debate over Missouri's future was the question of whether the U.S. Congress held the power to limit the existence of slavery. Slave supporters argued that it was a decision to be made by each state individually and exclusively. Northerners noted that the national government had already limited slavery. They looked back to the 1780s and the government under the Articles of Confederation that had established the Northwest Territory while banning slavery. This issue—the question of congressional power to restrict the expansion of slavery—would continue to create controversy for decades to follow.

Everyone expected a serious showdown when Congress came back into session in December. By then, however, the territory of Maine had applied for statehood as a free state. During

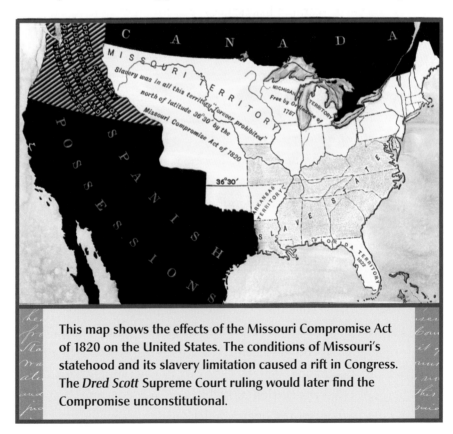

This map shows the effects of the Missouri Compromise Act of 1820 on the United States. The conditions of Missouri's statehood and its slavery limitation caused a rift in Congress. The *Dred Scott* Supreme Court ruling would later find the Compromise unconstitutional.

this session, Jesse B. Thomas, senator from Missouri's neighbor, Illinois, proposed an amendment allowing Missouri to enter the Union as a slave state, but closing slavery off to any future states carved out of the Louisiana Territory north of latitude 36 degrees, 30 minutes. (This east-west line was the southern border of Missouri. Missouri would be the only slave state to exist north of that line.) Months of debate passed until March 1820.

With the assistance of Kentucky Senator Henry Clay, an agreement was reached. It was known as the Missouri Compromise. Maine was admitted as a free state on March 15, 1820. Missouri was also allowed to adopt a state constitution that supported slavery. (The Tallmadge amendment was scrapped.) Statehood would not occur for Missouri until August 1821, however. When its new state constitution banned free blacks and people of mixed blood (having both black and white parents), Congress again intervened, declaring the constitution illegal, since it "abridged the privileges and immunities of U.S. citizens."[18] Another "Missouri Compromise" took place as Missouri agreed to drop the restriction. This entire process of bringing in Missouri as a slave state and Maine as free defined the future for slavery in the West. No slave states could be created out of the northern regions of the Louisiana Territory (by then called the Unorganized Territory and later the Nebraska Territory). Only one more state—Arkansas—was admitted with slavery inside its borders. By the 1820s, the end of slavery's expansion seemed established. Few Americans then could have foreseen what would happen just another generation later.

EQUAL JUSTICE UNDER LAW

3

A New Life
for Dred Scott

Although Dred Scott would one day become one of the most famous black slaves in American history, his origins are steeped in mystery. The exact year of his birth is in question. Historians are not even certain he should be called Dred Scott. A look at his background explains why this famous slave's beginnings are unertain, even to modern historians.

Existing records are unclear about when Dred Scott was born. Most indicate the year to be between 1795 and 1800. He was born in Southampton County, Virginia. Dred's first owners may have been a family named Scott. One of the family, a Virginia woman named Mary Scott, married a young man named Richard Blow in 1774 and went to live on one of the Blows' plantations known as Olde Place. The Blow family was a long-standing group of Virginia planters whose ancestors had first reached the colony during the 1600s. Early in her marriage to Richard, Mary gave birth to a son, Peter Blow. Tragically, Mary died in 1781, while Peter was quite young. Peter had been given some slaves before his mother's death. The parents of Dred Scott were probably among those slaves. According to the first record on the slave Scott, he was owned by Peter Blow. (According to some historians, the slave who would be known as Dred Scott may have actually been known as Sam as a young man. In 1833, when Peter Blow's estate was sold to pay off some debts, the sale bill listed a slave named Sam, but no Dred.)

Although Peter Blow, Dred's master, "was one of the least important and least wealthy of the Blows of Southampton County,"[19] the Blows were in general a significantly important and wealthy family. Peter was not exactly a poor man—he owned nearly 900 acres along the Gum Branch, a tributary of

This photograph of Dred Scott was taken in 1857, the year the Supreme Court decided whether he would be regarded as a person or property.

the Nottoway River. He married a local woman named Elizabeth Taylor just before Christmas 1800. By 1804, Peter and Elizabeth had their first child, a son named Thomas Vaughan. It is likely that young Dred may have been a playmate for young Thomas. Other Blow children soon arrived: Elizabeth Rebecca in 1806 and twin boys, Richard Benjamin and William Taylor, in 1808. Then came Charlotte Taylor in 1810 and a final sister, Patsey, two years later. Young Dred may have been old enough by then to take care of the twins. He may have fed them, changed their diapers, and done other domestic chores. Dred even may have slept on the floor in the same room as the young boys, so he would always be available, day or night.

According to records, young Dred did not grow up to be a large man. He was short, small-framed, and slightly built. Whereas many of the slaves on the Blow plantations were lighter skinned, often having been the product of the Blow men having children with black slaves, he was extremely dark. Dred may have suffered from illness when he was young, which may have slowed his growth.

None of the three Blow boys lived into adulthood. William died as an infant, Thomas died at age four, and Richard the following year. With these deaths, their father, Peter Blow, began to consider his plantation, built near swampy land, to be an unhealthy place to live. He did not pack up immediately, though, for he was not as wealthy as his relatives. His slaves worked the lands surrounding Olde Place, but the farmland was tired and worn out, having been overplanted for years and sapped of its nutrients. (At that time, fertilizer was not commonly in use on American farms.) Meanwhile, Elizabeth gave birth to two more sons: Peter, named for his father, in 1814, and Henry Taylor three years later. Dred Scott may have either been in his late teens or early 20s by then and may have been too old to work as a house servant, helping care for young children. He may, instead, have already been sent out to work Peter Blow's struggling plantation fields.

Ultimately, despite his family's success as Virginia planters, Peter Blow could not make a success of it himself. Other Virginia planters had already packed up and moved their operations to new lands, those in the Old Southwest (the modern-day states of Mississippi and Alabama). One had written friends back in Virginia that "there has not been a single instance of any person settling in this country who has . . . not become wealthy in a few years."[20] Such words were exactly what Peter Blow wanted to hear. The land there was rich, untapped by extensive agriculture—land ready to produce an abundance of cotton. Blow, worn out from trying to make himself wealthy planting cotton on land that was equally worn out, sold out in Virginia and moved his family—his wife, Elizabeth, and their surviving children—from Southampton County to virgin territory in Alabama. The year was 1818.

LEAVING VIRGINIA

Dred (now a young man), together with Peter's other slaves, joined Blow and his family in beginning their new life in Alabama. Once the Blows reached the lands that Peter had purchased before leaving Virginia, the work of establishing a new plantation started. In Alabama, cotton sold for 25 cents a pound, a good price. Blow's slaves, probably including Dred, set out to plant scores of acres of cotton. In this place, Peter Blow could start a new life, one filled with hope and his own personal dreams of success.

Even in Alabama, though, Peter's luck was little more than bad. No sooner had he reached his new lands and made a home for himself and his family, than the national economy unraveled. In 1819, the country slipped into a serious depression. The word "depression" was not yet used by economists, and the downturn in the economy became known as the "Panic of 1819." The Napoleonic Wars in Europe had helped keep American farm prices, including for cotton, artificially high. With those wars over by 1815, it had taken only a few years before the prices of farm products dropped significantly, in part because of overproduction. Cotton that had been selling for 25 cents a pound fell to 15 cents, then 12. Peter Blow's bad luck refused to leave him.

He struggled along for the next few years, but establishing and operating a new plantation in Alabama took money. Only the very wealthy could build up a new farming operation without borrowing money, and Peter Blow had to borrow a lot of money. Slaves were expensive; a good, strong, young field hand could cost as much as $500. There were the costs of feeding and clothing slaves, of buying land, of investing in livestock, and other expenses. And then, there were additional family expenses. Elizabeth Blow gave birth to another child, a boy named Taylor. Not long after another son was born, whom they named William Thomas. Almost immediately after Peter Blow arrived in Alabama, he was borrowing money heavily. By 1821, he was in debt for thousands of dollars, a lot of money in the early nineteenth century.

Throughout the 1820s, the Blow family continued to struggle with debt. In 1821, needing quick money, Peter borrowed $2,000 and put up eight of his slaves, including Dred, as collateral. If he defaulted on his loan, he would lose several, perhaps all of his slaves. By the next spring, it appears Peter may have been forced to surrender two of his slaves, but not Dred. In addition, Peter Blow took out new loans that spring, still needing ready cash. Nothing seemed to work for him. By December 1822, he was forced to sell his land for $5,000, enough to cover his debts, but leaving him little to show for his efforts.

Again, Blow uprooted his family and moved them, this time to a thriving, southern frontier town only three years old, situated on the banks of the Tennessee River—Florence, Alabama. But this time, Blow did not buy farmland and try his hand at running a third plantation. Instead, he invested in land in the town itself. Florence was growing quickly, and profits in real estate could bring significant profits to investors. Blow chose a property and rented a large house located in the heart of the booming town. He soon opened an establishment he named the Peter Blow Inn. Blow was tired of farming and failing. He would give the hotel business a go.

As for Blow's slaves, including Dred, their lives changed as the Blows made their move to Florence. Older male slaves carried luggage for the inn's guests. Others cooked or did laundry. Dred now found himself living in a busy Alabama town, laboring as a hostler, taking care of the horses that belonged to the guests at his master's inn. As a new innkeeper, Peter Blow did not need all of his slaves to work in his establishment. He hired some of them out to other plantation masters, which helped bring in extra money. Blow needed the money more now than he needed labor from those slaves.

Good fortune finally came to the Blow family. Peter's inn was an instant success, providing him with funds to invest further in Florence's real estate market. He bought additional town lots. A lot he bought one year for $600 would be sold just two or three years later for $2,000. Times were good for Florence, Alabama, and Peter Blow's family. He had found his place in the southern frontier, not as a planter but as a successful hotel operator. It would have made good sense for Blow to remain in Florence and continue running his profitable inn. But Florence was not growing fast enough for him. He decided he needed to pack up one more time and move to a larger city, one where he could make more money and become wealthy, which had been his lifelong goal. He made the decision in 1830 to move to the most exciting, bustling city on the American frontier—St. Louis, Missouri.

DRED AND ST. LOUIS

St. Louis had only become an American town a generation earlier, as part of the Louisiana Purchase. Prior to that, it had been a French trading town, established during the 1760s. When the Blow family, with their slaves in tow, arrived at the important

Mississippi River town, St. Louis was already considered the "Gateway to the West." Every year, hundreds of steamboats and keelboats tied up at its landings, loading and unloading great cargoes of goods. Among the items these boats delivered to the city were black slaves. Buying a house on Pine Street, located west of Main Street, Peter Blow opened up his new boarding establishment, naming it the Jefferson Hotel. Once again, Dred became the inn's hostler.

Peter Blow hoped his St. Louis hotel would be as successful as his inn in Florence had been. It would not prove to be so, however. Although Blow's business was not failing, he often found himself short on cash—a lifelong problem for him. The former Alabama planter soon realized he did not need as many slaves as he had owned in Florence. Without having enough available work for his black servants, Blow again hired some of them out. From time to time, this included Dred, who was hired out to work as a deckhand on steamboats. Consequently, Dred made many steamboat trips up and down the great Mississippi River.

Although this arrangement brought Blow some needed cash, he was not ultimately satisfied. In addition, his innkeeping business did not make him much money. He made up his mind that he would sell several of his young male slaves, including Dred Scott. These were slave men in their prime and would bring the best price in a sale of any that Blow owned. The lackluster success of his inn had first prompted him to sell several slaves, but other family events sped up the process. Blow's wife, Elizabeth, died during the summer of 1831, after lingering with a long-term disease. Then, one of Blow's daughters decided to marry. Both the funeral and the wedding were costly for Blow, causing him even bigger money problems.

What happened next with Dred Scott is still a mystery, as records are incomplete. It appears that a St. Louis physician, Dr. John Emerson, placed a down payment on the purchase of Dred Scott during the summer of 1831, when Blow's wife was ill. The amount of money in question does not appear to have

TAYLOR BLOW
AND DRED SCOTT

Dr. Emerson purchased Dred Scott either in 1832 or 1833, but that would not mark the last time Dred Scott would have any connection with the Blow family. During the years 1846–1847, when Scott's case was being litigated, the Blow family and their in-laws were among his most important supporters. He was especially supported by Taylor Blow, who would have been a young boy of 12 or so when Dred was sold.

What kind of relationship existed between Dred and young Taylor? The records are not clear. Perhaps Dred helped raise Taylor, as he had some of the older Blow children. Perhaps the two—white planter child and black slave—became close friends, even if the friendship was based on the responsibilities handed to Dred, which were those expected of him as a slave-servant. If that was the case, young Taylor was probably affected emotionally when Dred was sold to Dr. Emerson and left the Blow household.

One story concerning the Blow family and Dred Scott at the time of Scott's decade-long legal battle has been told repeatedly: Dred and his family, which included his wife and a child, had been abandoned by their owner in 1846, and the Blow family was providing their sole support. With this financial responsibility, the Blows supported Dred's lawsuit, hoping to "free themselves from the burden of supporting slaves that belonged to someone else."* This story appears to have been fiction. Dred Scott was not dependent on the charity of the Blows before filing his lawsuit. In addition, for the Blows to help Scott gain his freedom, they would not likely have become free of at least some responsibility for Dred and his family's livelihood.

---

* Quoted in Don E. Fehrenbacher, *The Dred Scott Case: Its Significance in American Law & Politics.* New York: Oxford University Press, 1978, p. 21.

been enough for Dred's outright purchase. It also appears that the complete sale of Dred was not made until 1833. Complicating matters was the death of Peter Blow on June 23, 1832. Whether Blow had completed the sale of his slave to Emerson or the sale was completed by one of Blow's daughters after her father's death, remains uncertain. The results were still the same, however. Dred Scott, who had always known life within the Blow household, found himself a young man in his early 30s owned by a stranger. However the purchase was finalized, Dred was not happy with his new circumstances. Separated from the Blow family and from the other slaves they owned, who were undoubtedly his friends, Dred ran away from Emerson and hid in a local swamp outside St. Louis. In time, he returned to Emerson, deciding to surrender to his new life.

As further evidence that slaves were considered pieces of property, owners were given receipts when purchasing them. The receipt shown here recorded a $250 payment by Judge Williams of Alabama, in exchange for a "Negro" man.

DRED SCOTT AND DR. EMERSON

At the time of Emerson's purchase of Dred Scott, the lives of both men were about to change significantly. Emerson had been trying to gain a position as an Army doctor. With a military of fewer than 10,000 men serving in peacetime, the Army had little need for medical officers. Emerson doggedly sought acceptance, however—calling on influential Missouri politicians, such as Senator Thomas Hart Benton, to support his application. By the time he purchased Scott, Dr. Emerson received the commission he had long sought. He was appointed as an assistant surgeon and assigned by the U.S. Army to take up his duties at Fort Armstrong, located at Rock Island, Illinois. Both doctor and slave took passage on a steamboat up the Mississippi River to the new post, arriving on December 1, 1833.

What, exactly, was the relationship between Dred Scott and his new owner initially is unclear. There are no records that indicate whether the two got along well or not or even liked each other. They were both about the same age, but the contrasts were significant. Naturally, one was a white owner and the other a black slave. In addition, Emerson was well educated, a doctor of medicine with a degree from the University of Pennsylvania, which he received in 1824. Scott, on the other hand, was illiterate and remained so all his life. (When signing legal documents, Scott wrote an 'X' for his signature.) Emerson moved to St. Louis in 1831 after spending some time in the South. During the fall of 1832, the regular medical officer at the nearby Jefferson Barracks fell ill and had to be replaced. Emerson took the job for a $100 monthly salary. The local quartermaster's office explained hiring a civilian for the job by claiming "no competent physician could be obtained . . . at a lower rate."[21] Emerson enjoyed the regular pay of working as an Army doctor and began applying for a medical officer's commission.

With Emerson's move to Illinois, Dred Scott suddenly found himself living outside the region of the country where slavery existed. Illinois had always been free territory, at least from 1787 and the passage of the Northwest Ordinance. This meant that, by law, slavery did not exist in Illinois, yet Emerson had brought his slave into the state, not simply while traveling through, but to take up residence. Whether or not Scott understood at the time that he was living in a free state is not known. Emerson certainly understood this but chose to bring his slave into Illinois anyway. Such a move did not immediately raise questions. It was common for military officers to keep slaves or personal servants no matter where they were posted. In fact, the federal government provided stipends to such officers to help defray the costs of feeding and clothing such black servants.

There would be no questions asked in Illinois. That state, despite its "free" status, was never a significant advocate of black rights, and the majority of the state's white population did not believe in black equality. Slaves brought there, especially for short visits, could not expect the Illinois courts to support them if they claimed they were automatically free. In general, though, "the state did not allow slavery or allow slaves to be kept there for long periods of time."[22] At the same time, the state did not go out of its way to pursue such cases and, in this case, Scott himself did not pursue any legal recourse:

> In the 1830s some Illinois attorneys were willing to fight for a slave's freedom even if the slave had no money to pay them, but such activist attorneys were not found in the remote area around Fort Armstrong. It is also possible that Dred Scott had no strong interest in seeking his freedom at that time, in that place. He may have found Dr. Emerson a tolerable master and felt that freedom on the Illinois frontier was not terribly advantageous. But most likely Scott failed to assert a claim to freedom while in Illinois because as an illiterate slave on an isolated army base he never learned that he could become free.[23]

Emerson had no need to worry about the issue. He did not intend to remain in Illinois for long. Nearly from the day he first set foot in Fort Armstrong, he was not happy there, and he began to request a different post almost immediately.

The move to another fort did not come for at least two years, however. During that time, Scott worked for his master, at first in the fort's hospital. Emerson found the hospital unsanitary, though, and requested permission to remove his patients into temporary tent shelters, until a new medical room could be built. He put Dred to work erecting the tents. When Emerson bought some local land outside the fort in the nearby town of Bettendorf, Iowa, he had Dred take up residence there to build a cabin on the new property.

By the spring of 1836, the Army ordered Fort Armstrong closed. This meant a new posting for Dr. Emerson and yet another move for Dred Scott. Emerson was assigned to Fort Snelling, located in Indian country, land that was then part of the Michigan Territory. (This territory would eventually be divided to create the states of Wisconsin, Minnesota, Iowa, and the Dakotas. As for Fort Snelling, it was located on the upper Mississippi River, near the site that would one day be St. Paul, Minnesota.) At the time, Scott was, perhaps, in his mid-30s. He had lived in Virginia, Alabama, Missouri, and, most recently, Illinois. As he and his master boarded the steamboat *Missouri Fulton*, he did not know what to expect to find in his new northern home.

The Further Travels of Dred Scott

4

At Fort Snelling, Dred Scott continued to find himself living where slavery was not legally recognized. Originally part of Michigan Territory, the region became part of the Wisconsin Territory between 1836 and 1838, after which it became the Iowa Territory, which was part of the old Louisiana Purchase. The lands where Scott lived in both Illinois and in Minnesota were free and never open to slavery. Scott, then, "who had been held as a slave in a free state for more than two years, was now taken into an area where slavery was forbidden by the Missouri Compromise" which had "forever prohibited" slavery in that region of the United States.[24]

YET ANOTHER MOVE

To drive the point even further, just two weeks before Emerson and his slave set out from Fort Armstrong for the doctor's new post, the U.S. Congress passed the Wisconsin Enabling Act of 1846, which created the Wisconsin Territory. The act confirmed that the Missouri Compromise, with its requisite ban on slavery, was still in effect. In addition, the new act put more teeth in the law limiting slavery in this region. The act's Section 12 stated that settlers in this territory would have the benefit of all the "rights, privileges, and advantages, granted and secured" by the 1787 Northwest Ordinance (which had denied slavery coming into the Old Northwest) and be "subject to all the conditions and restrictions and prohibitions" of that ordinance, including its nearly 50-year ban on slavery. The Wisconsin Enabling Act also stated that the laws of Michigan would be applied to the newly organized territory. By Michigan law, slavery had been

Situated in remote Illinois, Fort Armstrong was part of a free state. The relocation of Dred Scott to Illinois by Dr. Emerson would seem to be enough to change the slave's status to freedman, but the state did not actively enforce its antislavery laws.

The case of *Rachel v. Walker* (another misspelling) allowed for an enslaved woman to be freed because she had moved with her master to St. Louis, a territory where slavery was not legal. This petition was filed to stop Rachael's owner from taking her out of the area before her case could be tried in the St. Louis Circuit Court.

banned. At work, then, were three individual, yet overlapping assurances that slavery should not be recognized in the territory into which Dr. Emerson was taking his slave: the Missouri Compromise, the Northwest Ordinance of 1787, and the laws of Michigan. Yet Emerson introduced Scott to the region and caused him to live there for several years. To that end, during that time, "no military or civilian official ever tried to enforce the state and federal laws prohibiting slavery."[25]

There was some risk to white owners, even in the military, who brought their slaves into such free territory. Just a few years before Dred Scott's arrival at Fort Snelling, a case had come up, one that would later be cited as *Rachel v. Walker*. A slave woman named Rachel was brought to the fort as the property of an Indian subagent, Elias Langham. She was subsequently purchased by an army lieutenant who left Fort Snelling for reassignment in St. Louis. Having lived in free territory, Rachel took her case to court, claiming that, since she had been taken by her master to Fort Snelling to live, where slavery did not legally exist, she was automatically freed. The court decision came down in June 1836, a month after Emerson and Scott arrived at the northern post. The court agreed with Rachel's claim and granted her freedom; it also granted freedom to her young child. (The child had been delivered at Fort Snelling by the doctor Emerson would later replace.) Whether Dred Scott was aware of Rachel's case or not, is not clear.

A WIFE FOR DRED SCOTT

When the *Missouri Fulton* reached the site of Fort Snelling, Dred Scott saw "a glimmering-white, limestone-walled fort. And above Fort Snelling's grassy parade ground the stars and stripes flew, marking a tiny American outpost on Indian land."[26] Scott had traveled 700 miles northward, from St. Louis. When he arrived at the fort, the weather was cold, even for May. Dr. Emerson's new post was in a remote wilderness area. The fort was undermanned. Its construction had been completed in 1825, more than a decade earlier, and it had been built to house many more troops than it did in 1836. Although the fort may have been home to only a handful of troops, it was surrounded by many more Indians, who lived on the adjacent lands. Once Dred Scott took up residence at Fort Snelling, he realized he was not the only slave present. The fort was home to perhaps as many as 15 or 20 other slaves, most of whom were owned by Army officers such as Dr. Emerson. Dred had the opportunity to know all of them and become friends with many.

Probably still unaware that he was a slave living in a territory where slavery was illegal, Dred Scott continued to serve his master, Dr. Emerson. Life at Fort Snelling was different than any place Scott had ever lived, however. Outside the confines of the post, the woods teemed with wild animals, including bears. (Ten had been shot in the vicinity of the fort during the year prior to Scott's arrival.) The fort also housed an Indian agent, Major Lawrence Taliaferro, whose responsibility was to keep the local Indians passive. (Despite his name's spelling, it was pronounced "Tolliver.") Given Taliaferro's presence at the fort, Dakota Indians came and went with regularity. This might have been Scott's first contact with Native Americans. Some of those who visited the fort were "splendidly equipt with beautiful head dress & other ornaments of dress."[27] Scott had certainly landed in a world inhabited by strange and exotic residents.

Despite the novelties provided by Dakota Indians, wild animals, and the chills of living near modern-day St. Paul, Minnesota, Dred Scott had other distractions soon after arriving at the fort. Scott met a young slave girl named Harriet Robinson, who was owned by the Indian agent, Taliaferro. She had been brought to the fort a few years before Scott's arrival. Like Scott, she had lived in Virginia. She had also lived in Dedford, Pennsylvania (a free state), while owned by Taliaferro, before being brought out to Fort Snelling. She was much younger than Dred, perhaps no more than 17 years old. Scott was possibly more than twice her age. As an Indian agent, Taliaferro's residence was outside the fort, but this did not keep Scott from mingling with Taliaferro's slaves, including Harriet.

Little is known of Harriet's life before she met Dred Scott. As a slave, she would not have had a legal last name, only Harriet. However, Major Taliaferro would later identify her as Harriet Robinson. Where the name came from is unclear, but Harriet used it as an adult. It may have been the name of the Virginia planter family who had owned Harriet's mother or the name of Harriet's owners before her purchase by Major Taliaferro. (There was, in fact, a Robinson family that had been close neighbors to the Taliaferros, in Virginia.)

Sometime between May 1836 and the fall of 1837, Dred Scott and Harriet Robinson were married. Major Taliaferro officiated over the ceremony, because he was a justice of the peace, but the union of these two was more complicated than it would appear. By law, slave marriages were not recognized. Also, if slaves did engage in some marriage ritual, they could not become husband and wife while owned by two different masters. Because each was the property of someone else, an official transfer of "property rights" had to accompany such a marriage union. It appears that, either Major Taliaferro sold Harriet to Emerson or simply gave her to Dred to marry with no strings attached. (Records indicate that, following their marriage, Dred and Harriet were referred to as "Dr. Emerson's slaves.") It would be a marriage that would last more than 20 years, until the death of Dred Scott. Dred and Harriet produced four children, two sons and two daughters. Although the sons died in infancy, the daughters lived into adulthood. When Dred Scott filed his lawsuit to gain his freedom, he filed it not only in his name, but in Harriet's and his daughters' names, as well.

RETURNING TO SLAVE COUNTRY

Although Dred Scott had found ways to cope with his new life in the north, Dr. Emerson struggled through his first winter there and decided he did not like the post. In the spring of 1837, Emerson wrote to the surgeon general that the harsh Minnesota winter had left him miserable with rheumatism, and he asked for reassignment back to St. Louis. His request was granted. By the following October, he left Fort Snelling for Jefferson Barracks in St. Louis. Emerson did not immediately take his two slaves with him, however. They remained at Fort Snelling, where they were hired out by Emerson to other officers, who would pay them for their work. Two months later, Emerson was reassigned further south to Fort Jesup, Louisiana, on the border between Louisiana and Texas. Emerson was still unsatisfied with his post, so much so that he requested a return to

Fort Snelling! At the fort, however, Emerson did meet a young woman named Eliza Irene Sanford, age 23, the younger sister of the wife of a Lieutenant Henry Bainbridge and daughter of a wealthy Virginia manufacturer. Following a brief courtship, Emerson and Eliza—everyone called her "Irene"—married on February 6, 1838.

Not long after Dr. Emerson's wedding, he summoned Dred and Harriet to Louisiana; the couple probably took passage on a Mississippi steamboat during the spring of 1838. Dred and Harriet rejoined Emerson and his new wife in Louisiana, but they did not remain there for long. By October, the doctor's request for yet another transfer was approved, and once again, Emerson and his slaves were back at Fort Snelling. Dred was again living in free territory. Emerson booked his party's passage on a small, sternwheeler steamboat, *Gypsy*. During the trip up the Mississippi, Harriet gave birth to their first child, whom the slave couple named Eliza, after Dr. Emerson's new wife. Although, by law, the infant Eliza was a slave, she "was born on a boat in the Mississippi River, surrounded on one side by the free state of Illinois and on the other side by the free territory of Wisconsin."[28] Emerson, his wife, and the Scotts reached Fort Snelling on October 21.

Despite having practically begged to be reassigned at Fort Snelling, Dr. Emerson was not happy following his return to the northern fort. In 1839, Emerson quarreled with the quartermaster over the latter's refusal to provide a heating stove the doctor had ordered for Dred Scott and his wife. The argument turned into a scuffle, and Emerson was struck in the face, which broke his glasses. When Emerson returned to the fray, he was brandishing two pistols, which sent the quartermaster running for his life. By the following year, Emerson was reassigned to yet another military post, this time in Florida. As the post was in the heart of Seminole Indian country, and the federal government was fighting a war with the Seminoles, Emerson elected to leave his wife and the Scotts in St. Louis to live. Still not satisfied with his posting, the doctor filed for yet another transfer. He complained, as he always did, of poor health. When two junior officers were reassigned to Washington, D.C., ahead of him, he fired off an angry letter to the surgeon general. Tiring of Dr. Emerson's endless complaints and constant stream of transfer requests, the Army decided to cut him from the service, giving him an honorable discharge from military duty in August 1842.

THE BRITISH PRECEDENT FOR FREEING SLAVES

Although important American legal cases such as *Winny v. Whitesides* and others set the precedents necessary for Dred Scott to file his suit with great expectations of winning his freedom, those cases had their own precedents. One important foundational case regarding the freeing of slaves based on free residence wasn't an American case at all. It took place under British law.

This significant, ground-breaking case was cited as *Somerset v. Stewart* and dated from 1772, even before the establishment of the United States as a nation. In its simplest terms, Somerset was a slave who was owned in colonial Virginia, then taken to England. There, Somerset ran away from his master, only to be recaptured and consigned to a ship's captain, to be sold in Jamaica.

When Somerset was brought before the King's Bench (an English court), however, he was ordered released by the presiding judge, Lord Mansfield, who ruled that, since England had no specific laws defining and regarding slavery on its soil, then Somerset was a free man. In other words, slavery did not explicitly exist in Great Britain. In addition, Mansfield ruled that the institution of slavery was one "so contrary to the common law and natural law that only the enactment of specific legislation could support it."* The decision's bottom line was this: When a slave was introduced into a place lacking laws in support of

Emerson packed his bags and made his way back west to St. Louis to be reunited with his wife. During the two and a half years Emerson was in Florida, Dred Scott worked for Emerson's wife, Irene. While in St. Louis, Dred was also able to make contact with some of the children of Peter and Elizabeth Blow, who were adults by that time. It was probably during these years that Taylor Blow reunited with Dred Scott.

---

slavery, the slave automatically became a free person. *Somerset v. Stewart* would remain the most important precedent for deciding American cases for the next 70 years.

On the other hand, whereas Somerset helped establish the "once free, forever free" rule, another British case amended it. In an 1827 case, *The Slave, Grace*, the English High Court of Admiralty altered the Somerset decision, establishing the concept of reversion. In this case, a West Indian slave named Grace had been taken from her Caribbean home to England, then returned to Antigua at a later date. After reaching Antigua, Grace sued for her freedom, claiming that England did not have slavery and while there she was free. This time, however, the court decided against the slave. The court stated that Grace's residence in England merely suspended her status as a slave temporarily. Once Grace was returned to Antigua, the "law of England would no longer be in force and the person's status would once again be determined by the laws of the slave jurisdiction."** Both cases would play an important role in the outcome of the Dred Scott decision.

---

* Quoted in Paul Finkelman, *Dred Scott v. Sandford: A Brief History With Documents*. Boston: Bedford Books, 1997, p. 20.
** Ibid., p. 21.

The back of this photograph reads, "copied from an old civil war photograph found among my mother's things...Dred Scott belonged to my great Aunt Irene...white man unknown...Christine Baker Rowell."

In typical fashion, Dr. Emerson was no more happy in St. Louis, out of military service, than he had been with his string of disappointing postings over the previous decade. He could not seem to get a private practice established. He thought his only hope was to get back into the Army and become a military surgeon again. Before receiving word on his request for a new Army commission, Emerson and his wife moved to Davenport, Iowa, a newly established frontier settlement. There, the doctor attempted to establish a practice, bought and sold real estate, and began construction on a new brick house. His wife, Irene, was pregnant by then. As for Dred and Harriet, they had been left in St. Louis, again hired out to work for others, with Emerson receiving the money. Irene gave birth to a baby girl named Henrietta in November 1842. Then, tragedy struck. A month later, on December 29, Dr. Emerson, who had struggled for years with illnesses both real and imagined, died at age 40.

Although the actual cause of his death may have been some other ailment, Emerson officially died of consumption, known today as tuberculosis. When Emerson died, Dred Scott and his wife were still living in St. Louis.

THE LAST WILL AND TESTAMENT OF JOHN EMERSON

As John Emerson lay dying, he organized his affairs in the form of a will. That such a document existed at his death would be extremely crucial to Dred Scott's application for his freedom in just a few years. According to the will, Dr. Emerson left his entire estate, including lands and slaves, to his wife, "during the term of her natural life."[29] At her death, Emerson's estate was to pass to his daughter, Henrietta. But the will did not intend for Emerson's property to be held as a "trust" for Henrietta. (If Emerson had left his property as a trust to his daughter until she reached a specific age as an adult, then Emerson's wife would have been obligated to hold all property until that date.) This is not what Emerson stipulated in his will. Instead, he authorized Irene to sell any of his property to provide an income for her and their infant daughter. To make certain the will's stipulations were met, Dr. Emerson had appointed John F. A. Sanford, his wife's brother, as executor. John Sanford "failed to qualify as executor in Iowa,"[30] however. Instead, Irene Emerson's father, Alexander Sanford, was appointed by the courts to serve as the estate administrator. He did not fully carry out his duties as executor before he died in 1848, however.

Irene Emerson, then, was fully empowered to execute her husband's estate, according to his will. In its specifics, the will mentioned 19 acres of land owned by Emerson and some furniture. Unfortunately, Emerson's will did not mention his slaves and what should happen to them. Irene Emerson retained control of them, though, and chose to hire them out in St. Louis for three years following her husband's death, just as Emerson himself had done. While Harriet and Eliza Scott remained in

St. Louis, Dred was hired to Irene Emerson's brother-in-law, U.S. Army Captain Henry Bainbridge, a graduate of West Point Military Academy. In 1843, after serving in Florida, Bainbridge had been assigned to Jefferson Barracks, near St. Louis.

Again, Dred found himself serving a military officer. He accompanied Bainbridge to Fort Jesup in 1844 and the next year went to Texas with the captain, which had just been annexed into the United States. In 1846, Harriet gave birth to a second daughter, Lizzie, while she was working and living at the Jefferson Barracks. That same year, in February, Dred was sent back to St. Louis by Irene Emerson. (By then, Captain Bainbridge was preparing to enter service in the Mexican War.) Soon after his return to the Mississippi River town, Dred was hired out to work for a local man named Samuel Russell. About that time, though, Dred was making overtures to Irene Emerson concerning his freedom and that of his family. He offered Mrs. Emerson $300 as a down payment of sorts. Irene Emerson, however, was not interested in Dred Scott's offer. Then, to Irene's surprise, Dred Scott and his wife, Harriet, took a bold step, one that would set the course for the remainder of Dred's life. On April 6, 1846, the Scotts filed a petition in the Missouri Circuit Court of St. Louis. They were suing Irene Emerson for their freedom and for the freedom of their two daughters, Eliza and Lizzie.

EQUAL·JUSTICE·UNDER·LAW·

5

Scott v. Emerson

The Scotts had decided to take a bold step in the spring of 1846 and file a suit for their freedom and for that of their two children. In fact, the Scotts' attorney, Francis B. Murdoch, filed two suits in St. Louis court, *Dred Scott versus Irene Emerson* and *Harriet Scott versus Irene Emerson.* In the motion filed in Dred's name on April 6, the legal document stated that Scott was "entitled to his freedom."[31] Both suits claimed that Dred and Harriet had been held against their will and that Irene Emerson was guilty of false imprisonment. According to the Scotts' claim, just two days before filing their suits, on April 4, "Mrs. Emerson had 'beat, bruised and ill-treated' Dred and had imprisoned him for twelve hours."[32] Dred's case asked for a payment of ten dollars for damages. The wording of Harriet's claim against Irene Emerson was similar. In time, Harriet's case was dropped, with the understanding that whatever the outcome of her husband's case, it would apply to her as well.

THE CASE FOR FREEDOM

Little is known about Dred and Harriet Scott's first attorney, Francis Murdoch. It is unclear how he came to be involved in the case. Although he was known for his opposition to slavery, he was not known to be a lawyer who filed freedom cases for

To the Hon. John M. Krum, Judge of the St. Louis Circuit Court

Dred Scott, a man of color, respectfully states to your honor, that he is claimed as a slave by one Irene Emerson, of the County of St. Louis, State of Missouri, widow of the late Dr. John Emerson, who at the time of his death was a surgeon in the United States army. That said Dr. John Emerson purchased your petitioner in the city of St. Louis about nine years ago, he then being a slave, from one Peter Blow now deceased and took petitioner with him to Rock Island in the State of Illinois, and there kept petitioner to labor and service in attendance upon said Emerson, for about two years and six months, he the said Emerson being attached to the United States troops there stationed as surgeon. That after remaining at the place last named for about the period aforesaid, said Emerson was removed from the garrison at Rock Island aforesaid, to Fort Snelling on the St Peters river in the territory of Iowa, and took petitioner with him, at which latter place he petitioner continued to remain in attendance upon said Dr John Emerson doing labor and service, for a period of about five years. That after the lapse of the period last named, said Emerson was ordered to Florida, and proceeding thence left petitioner at Jefferson Barracks in the County of St Louis aforesaid in charge of one Capt. A. Bainbridge to whom said Emerson hired Petitioner. That said Emerson is now dead, and his widow the said Irene claims petitioner's services as a slave, and as his owner, but believing that under this state of facts, that he is entitled to his freedom he prays your honor to allow him to sue said Irene Emerson in said Court, in order to establish his right to freedom & he will pray &c.

Dred Scott
his mark

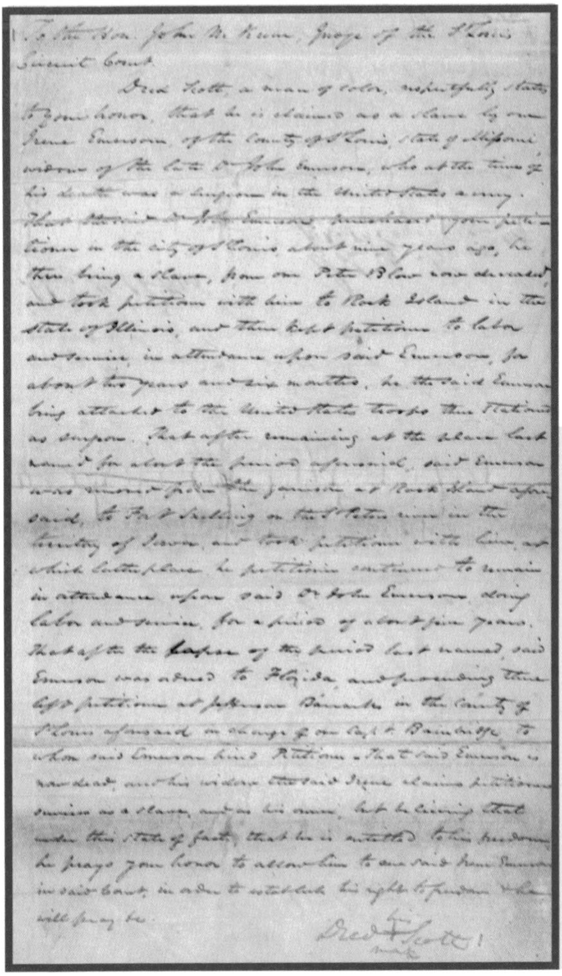

The first page of Dred Scott's November 1846 petition to sue for his freedom is shown at left. At that stage, the case was known as Dred Scott, a man of color, v. Irene Emerson. Notice Scott's mark at the lower right corner of the document.

slaves. Perhaps a portion of his motivation came from Reverend John Anderson. Apparently, Anderson and Murdoch had both lived in Alton, Illinois, during the 1830s, when the antislavery newspaper publisher Elijah P. Lovejoy was killed during a riot provoked by angry, proslavery supporters. Perhaps through some longstanding connection between the two of them, Anderson the minister was able to convince Murdoch the lawyer to work on behalf of the Scotts. On the other hand, they may only have met more recently in St. Louis. The answer to Murdoch's motivation remains unknown. He did not stick with the case, however; he resigned and left St. Louis before the Dred Scott case even went to court.

According to the legal papers filed by Murdoch, Dred Scott claimed he should be freed because his previous master, Dr. John Emerson, had taken him into a state and territories where slavery did not legally exist, including his posts at Fort Armstrong, Illinois, and Fort Snelling, in the Wisconsin Territory. At the time of the filing of the two suits, Dred and Harriet's attorney had every expectation that the Scotts' case would be easy to win. There were, after all, similar cases that had already been decided that could serve as precedents for the Dred Scott case. In 1824, a parallel case, *Winny v. Whitesides*, had been decided by the Missouri Supreme Court in favor of a slave who had been taken into free territory by her owner Phoebe Whitesides. The origins of the case dated back to 1795, when the slave Winny was moved from the slave state of Kentucky by her owner to the Indiana Territory and took up residence there. Indiana was part of the Old Northwest, where slavery had always been illegal under the Northwest Ordinance of 1787. Subsequently, the Whitesides had moved to Missouri Territory, and it was there that Winny had filed a suit to gain her freedom. In their majority opinion, Justices Mathias McGirk and George Tompkins stated that "this court thinks that the person who takes his slave into said Territory and by the length of his residence there indicates an intention of making that place his residence & that of his slave and thereby induces a jury to believe that in fact does by such residence declare his slave to have become a free man."[33] The Winny case was one of the first to establish the legal precedent embodied in the phrase: "Once free, forever free."

In the 13 years following the *Winny v. Whitesides* decision, the Missouri court had heard as many as ten additional cases in which a slave sued for his or her freedom based on residence in a free region. Similar cases were also filed in Kentucky, Louisiana, and Mississippi, with similar results in favor of the slave filing the suit. Since during this period, "Missouri was one of the most liberal states in the nation on this question,"[34] based on the earlier precedents, Dred Scott and his attorney should have had every expectation that his case would be easily won.

That the Dred Scott filing accused Irene Emerson in harsh, strong words should not be interpreted as inherently hostile on the part of Dred Scott. Scott's attorney was following the established course of action required by Missouri statute:

> Missouri slave law, modeled after that of Virginia and Kentucky, had always included a chapter on suits for freedom.... A suit for freedom took the conventional form of a suit for damages in which it was understood that the alleged acts of the defendant were lawful chastisement [punishment] of a slave by his master but constituted assault and false imprisonment if the plaintiff were indeed a free man. Thus, the jury could not reach a verdict without first deciding on the validity of the plaintiff's claim to freedom.[35]

For Scott's attorneys, the task before them was fairly clear and simple. They only had to prove two points: (1) that Dred (and Harriet by connection) "had been taken to reside on free soil and that, (2) he was now claimed or held as a slave by Mrs. Emerson."[36] Producing witnesses needed to corroborate Dred's version of the details regarding residence at Forts Armstrong and Snelling would be easy enough to do. While the first point would be easy to prove, the second, ironically, would not.

There would be complications almost from the beginning of this case. The case moved slowly through the legal system once Mrs. Emerson and her attorneys decided they wanted to fight Dred's claim. Irene Emerson's pleas of "not guilty" were not filed for more than six months after Dred's suit was filed, on November 19, 1846. With the court's docket already full, the suit did not come to trial until June 30, 1847, more than a year after Dred's original filing.

THE TRIAL BEGINS

Dred Scott v. Sandford was tried in the "Old Courthouse," which still stands today in downtown St. Louis as a noteworthy historical landmark, nearly in the shadow of the city's Gateway Arch. The courthouse, which began construction in 1839, was a fairly new building at the time. During the first Dred Scott trial, it was not yet fully completed. (The specific room where the case was tried no longer exists; the interior of the courthouse has since been remodeled.) Judge Alexander Hamilton (no relation to the founding father of the same name) presided over the case. He was a new judge, a native of Philadelphia, and one whose "sympathy toward freedom suits was well known."[37] Murdoch was not present, as he had left the case, as well as St. Louis, by 1847. It appears that Dred's case was instead presented by Samuel Mansfield Bay, a former Missouri attorney general. George W. Goode, a Virginia lawyer who was also a strong pro-slavery supporter, represented Irene Emerson.

In the midst of those supporting Dred and Harriet Scott during this first trial were members of the Blow family whose father had once owned Scott. All the Blow children had grown up by then, and the young Blow men had become successful and prosperous, at least to some degree, though largely not as planters. Young Peter Blow was married, still living in St. Louis, his wife coming from a prominent family, the LaBeaumes. Charlotte Blow Charles (Dred had probably been sold years earlier to help pay for Charlotte's wedding) had convinced her

St. Louis's Old Courthouse was the site of Dred Scott's first two trials. Although the courtroom used for Scott's trials no longer exists, the courthouse still stands as one of St. Lousis' oldest buildings. Today the building is a museum and features exhibits on the Dred Scott case.

husband to employ her younger brothers in his business. Charlotte was, herself, an important and respected member of the St. Louis "upper crust." As for sister Patsey, she had married a lawyer named Charles Drake. Drake became directly involved in Dred Scott's case; he was one of the attorneys who took affidavits from those selected to testify on behalf of Dred. Although Drake's contribution was important, the Blow family was also providing financial assistance to Dred, their former slave, by helping cover the costs of the suit.

Attorney Bay opened his arguments by showing that Scott had, in fact, lived on free soil by having been taken by Emerson to his western fort postings. Several witnesses testified to that effect. Miles Clark was one witness. He had been posted at Fort Armstrong, in Illinois, and remembered that Dred "was claimed by Doctor Emerson as a slave and used by him as such."[38] The former wife of a Lieutenant Thompson, Catherine Anderson, was present and testified that she had hired Harriet from Dr. Emerson in 1837 at Fort Snelling. By her testimony, she claimed that the Scotts were "universally known there to be Dr. Emerson's Slaves."[39]

There would be problems with proving that Dred Scott was, indeed, owned by Mrs. Emerson, however. It was clear to everyone familiar with the case that Irene Emerson was Dred and Harriet's owner. The problem was in proving it. When attorneys called Samuel Russell to the stand, Russell did admit he had hired the Scotts from Mrs. Emerson to work, but that he had paid the money not to Irene Emerson, but to her father, Alexander Sanford. When Scott's attorneys cross-examined Russell, he admitted that it was his wife, not he, who had handled the arrangements to hire the Scotts and that he had done nothing but pay the money to Sanford. In further testimony, Henry T. Blow testified that his father, Peter Blow, had originally sold Dred Scott to Dr. John Emerson. *Dr. Emerson* was not *Mrs. Emerson*, however. By the end of a single day of testimony, the case was decided against Dred Scott. Thus, the original trial regarding Dred Scott's application for freedom was decided on an ironic technicality: "The decision produced the absurd effect of allowing Mrs. Emerson to keep her slaves simply because no one had proved that they *were* her slaves."[40] Unfortunately, Dred and Harriet Scott had waited a year for their case to be heard and had lost in a strange twist of events.

CALLING FOR A NEW TRIAL

Dred's attorneys immediately called for a new trial. Russell's awkward testimony had caught them by surprise. On July 1, 1847, the day following the court's ruling against Dred Scott, petitions were filed to establish a second set of suits on behalf of Dred and Harriet, this time against Irene Emerson, Alexander Sanford, and Samuel Russell. The strategy was clear. Attorneys intended to circle their legal wagons around the three individuals who may have held the Scotts as slaves. But the Scotts would have to again wait until it was time to place their new case on the docket of the Missouri court system. It would not be until December 2, 1847, that Judge Hamilton granted motions for a retrial. (By then, the suit filed against Sanford, Emerson, and Russell had been dismissed as a "duplication" of the Scott's original suit against Mrs. Emerson alone.) At the same time, however, Mrs. Emerson's attorneys "filed a bill of exceptions to the order for a new trial."[41]

Between trials, where were Dred and Harriet Scott? Since they claimed to be free, Mrs. Emerson could not hold them until the courts made a ruling. In the meantime, she turned them over to the local sheriff for safekeeping. Irene Emerson told the sheriff he was free to hire them out, but he was to keep the money until the court handed down a ruling. As for the Scott children, Eliza and Lizzie, Harriet hid them with friends, but did not tell anyone where they were. Again, the Blow family intervened. Peter Blow's brother-in-law, an attorney named C. Edmund LaBeaume, hired Dred and Harriet. During the years of legal proceedings, the Scotts were forced to put their lives and their family on hold.

Dred and Harriet's case had been transferred to the law firm of Alexander P. Field and David N. Hall. As for Mrs. Emerson, attorney Goode was still working on her behalf. Dred could not have had a greater legal advocate than Alexander Field. He was an expert trial attorney. The new trial, the one stemming from Mrs. Emerson's appeal, did not open until April, 1848. By June, the Missouri Supreme Court had handed down a decision. It was anticlimatic. The court dismissed the writ of error filed by Mrs. Emerson and called for yet another trial, which did not convene for another year and a half. Judge William Scott, writing for the highest state court, declared that "since a new trial had already been ordered . . . there was no final judgment upon which a writ of error could lie."[42] Trial dates were set twice, both in February and May, 1849, then cancelled and rescheduled. Why this happened is not clear, but these postponements may have been the result of two catastrophes that struck St. Louis that spring: a city-wide fire and a cholera epidemic.

A RETURN TO COURT

When the new trial was finally held, on January 12, 1850, Judge Alexander Hamilton was still presiding. The Scotts' attorneys soon cleared up all the confusion from the first trial, establishing that Mrs. Russell had hired the Scotts from their owner, Mrs. Emerson. Although Adeline Russell appeared as a witness, she did not perform much better in court than her husband had, stating under oath that "The only way I know these negroes belonged to Mrs. Emerson is that she hired them to me."[43] As for Mrs. Emerson, when the new trial opened, she was not present. In fact, she no longer lived in St. Louis, having remarried and moved to Springfield, Massachusetts. (Ironically, the woman who was fighting to keep ownership of two slaves had married an antislavery man, another doctor, named Calvin C. Chaffee, who would later be elected as a Massachusetts congressman.) Acting on Irene's behalf was her brother, John Sanford.

Defense attorneys had changed their approach for this new trial, arguing that Dr. Emerson, while serving in the Army as a doctor at Fort Armstrong and Snelling, had been working under the jurisdiction of the military and was not under the civil laws prohibiting slavery. This position, of course, did not take into consideration the *Rachel v. Walker* case. It also did not explain the fact that Emerson left his slaves at Fort Snelling after his departure and had left them to work for others. Once all testimony was delivered, Judge Hamilton gave instructions to the jury "in terms highly favorable to the plaintiff."[44] Then, the jury delivered its verdict: Dred Scott was a free man. After four years of legal proceedings flanked by lengthy postponements, the future for Dred and Harriet seemed bright.

Mrs. Emerson's attorneys were not prepared to surrender their case, however. At first, they tried to schedule another trial in Missouri court. That effort failed. Then, they attempted to bring the case for appeal before the Missouri Supreme Court. They filed their motion in March 1850, but the highest Missouri court postponed its decision to hear the case until 1852. The timing of the next hearing of the Dred Scott case would prove extremely crucial in light of what was going on regarding the question of expanding slavery in the United States. National events were likely playing against Dred Scott. Prior to 1850, the

WHAT THE SCOTTS KNEW AND HOW THEY CAME TO KNOW IT

In 1846, the year Dred Scott and his wife, Harriet, filed their suit to gain their freedom, the Scotts were living once again in St. Louis. Missouri was a slave state, yet Dred Scott chose to take legal action then, rather than when he was living in the free state of Illinois or the free territory of Wisconsin. The move seems ill-timed and belated. Why 1846, and in a court situated in a slave state?

The answer is not clear. Historians speculate that the illiterate Dred might not have been aware that he had a legal right to sue for his freedom while living in Illinois and the Wisconsin Territory. This is entirely possible. Also, it is possible that Emerson had verbally promised Dred Scott his freedom at some date prior to his death but had never acted on that promise. Scott's filing could have been spurred by Emerson's unfulfilled vow. There is no evidence of this, however.

It is possible that by the mid-1840s, Dred Scott simply came to understand his options in suing for freedom. With Emerson dead and his will failing to mention Emerson's slaves, the time may have just seemed right to file such a suit. It is possible that one of the Blow family explained to Dred the options he had available. That Taylor Blow became

Dred Scott case had drawn little significant attention outside St. Louis, specifically, and Missouri, in general. Other cases such as his and Harriet's had made their way through the courts in previous years, but between 1850 and 1852 a change in the course of the politics of slavery took place.

THE POLITICS OF SLAVERY

A series of events relevant to the Scott case could be dated back to as early as the spring of 1846. Within a month of the original filing of the Dred Scott case, the United States had gone to war

involved as Dred's sponsor and financial supporter during the years of legal action that followed is a matter of record.

It is also possible that Dred Scott did not come up with the idea of suing for his freedom, but that it came from his wife, Harriet. While living in St. Louis, Harriet attended the Second African Baptist Church, which was presided over by the Reverend John R. Anderson. Earlier in his life, Anderson had been a slave but had bought his freedom. As a young, free black man, he had been hired on as a typesetter for an abolitionist newspaper in Alton, Illinois, by its editor, Elijah P. Lovejoy. (In 1837, Lovejoy became a martyr for the cause of antislavery when he was murdered in Alton by a proslavery mob.) It may have been Reverend Anderson or another member of his congregation who came to know about Harriet and her husband having been held where slavery was banned.

How Dred Scott and Harriet came to understand their right to sue for their freedom may never be known, but one thing is clear: Once they decided to file their suit, they received support from many circles, including Taylor Blow and Reverend Anderson.

with Mexico, officially over the border between Mexico and the United States. As the war with Mexico unfolded that summer, legislation was created in the House of Representatives that earmarked monies to be used to transfer Mexican territory to the United States once the U.S. military won the war. On August 8, a representative from Pennsylvania, David Wilmot, attempted to amend the legislation by calling for a ban on slavery in any territory annexed from Mexico following the war. Wilmot's "proviso" did not sit well with southern slave supporters in Congress. They "regarded the Wilmot Proviso as an outrageous attempt to deprive them of their rightful share of the spoils of conquest."[45] The measure was defeated.

What followed was a further drawing of ideological battle lines between southerners who supported slavery's expansion into the West and northerners who hoped to limit the movement of slavery into new regions of the United States. In 1848, the presidential election was dominated by this slavery issue face-off. Then, in 1850, the Pacific Coast territory of California (part of the land the United States actually did gain after defeating Mexico) applied for statehood. The territory had "Americanized" quickly in the previous year, with the coming of the California Gold Rush and the emigration of thousands of U.S. citizens into the former Mexican-held territory. California intended to enter the Union as a free state, but southerners blocked its admittance, just as northerners had once attempted to block the admittance of Missouri as a slave state.

The result became known as the Compromise of 1850. (Just as Henry Clay had helped hammer out the Missouri Compromise almost 30 years earlier, he was also important in creating this new deal concerning slavery's future.) The compromise did allow California to become a free state, but southerners were promised that the remainder of the Mexican cession lands would remain open to slavery in the future. Also, southerners were appeased by the Compromise, which called for the writing of a new, stricter Fugitive Slave Law.

Through these few years, extending from the end of the Mexican War to the writing of the Compromise of 1850, southerners became more and more concerned about the future expansion of slavery:

> More than that, they were becoming convinced that any congressional restriction on slavery in the territories was a judgment on the morality of [slavery] and therefore degrading to the South. Feeding their anger and fear were … northern hostility in editorials, sermons, legislative resolutions, and fugitive slave "rescues." Southern attitudes accordingly hardened into a grim defensiveness, and, by 1850, the public mood of the slaveholding states was [not open to] to suits for freedom.[46]

Such a change in sympathy for cases such as Dred Scott's would prove difficult to overcome despite the merits of the case. As one historian summed things up: "The Scotts as suitors for freedom would become casualties of the sectional conflict."[47]

EQUAL·JUSTICE·UNDER·LAW·

6

Once Free, Forever Free?

That the Dred Scott case was unfolding in Missouri, specifically, only complicated matters. The state was in a precarious situation both geographically and historically. Since the Missouri Compromise had established slavery there, Missouri was a slave state surrounded "on three sides by free territory."[48] Unlike nearly all other southern slaveholding states, Missouri was home to a very vocal minority of antislavery advocates. As they spoke out against slavery, they only made the state's slaveholders more nervous.

A CONTINUING LEGAL BATTLE

Although southern Democrat leaders typically supported slavery, Missouri's Democrat leader, Thomas Hart Benton, had long ago put off southerners for his opposition to Texas' annexation; his political hostility toward the de facto southern supporter of slavery, John C. Calhoun of South Carolina; and his "moderate" views on the institution of slavery in general. By the fall of 1850, at least two of the three Missouri Supreme Court judges—James H. Birch and William B. Napton—had become anti-Benton men and proslavery advocates. They looked forward to the opportunity to hear the Dred Scott case. Birch hoped to use the case as a way of declaring the Missouri Compromise unconstitutional. Between the two proslavery justices, they were able to convince the court's third judge, John F. Ryland, a moderate on slavery, to agree with the ruling that Birch and Napton intended to make if, indeed, the Dred Scott case landed on their judicial doorstep.

Judge Napton was selected to write the Missouri Supreme Court's majority decision. Before he could do so, though, and after months of delaying (Napton kept claiming that he needed additional law books, those unavailable in the state library), politics intervened against him and his colleague, Judge Birch. A recent change in the Missouri Constitution had changed the status of the state's supreme court justices from an appointed position to an elected one. In September 1851, when elections were held, only Ryland was returned to the court. Napton and Birch were replaced. This political sweep of those on the court strongly opposed to Dred Scott gaining his freedom meant that the case would have to be tried once again by a new, reorganized court.

The two new Missouri Supreme Court justices to sit on the bench with incumbent judge Ryland were Hamilton R. Gamble and William Scott, no stranger to the Dred Scott case. Judge Scott had been on the state high court in 1848. Scott was also a proslavery advocate, though, and he was ready to pick up Napton's cause. As for Gamble, he, too, was not unfamiliar with slave freedom cases. He had represented the slaveholding army officer in the *Rachel v. Walker* case, years earlier.

 ONE CASE IMPACTS ANOTHER

As the three judges who comprised the Missouri Supreme Court con-sidered the legitimacy of Dred Scott's claim that he was no longer a slave, but a free man, another case was making its way through the United States Supreme Court. This case—*Strader v. Graham*—would im-pact the decision rendered by the Missouri justices.

The background for *Strader v. Graham* is typical, yet unique. The case rose out of Kentucky, where some slave musicians had been taken into the free states of Ohio and Indiana to perform. In time, these same slaves escaped from Kentucky to freedom in Canada. When a suit was filed in Kentucky court, it was not to regain the escaped slaves, but to sue several individuals who had helped the slaves escape. In defend-ing the accused, lawyers argued that the slaves who had escaped were not actually slaves at all, for they had become free men when taken on northern, free soil. Not only were the states of Ohio and Indiana free, but the original territory, known as the Old Northwest, had never been open to slavery under the Northwest Ordinance of 1787. When the Kentucky Court of Appeals decided against the accused in favor of the slaveowner, the case then moved to the United States Supreme Court under a *writ of error*.

When the case reached the desk of the Chief Justice, Roger B. Taney, he dismissed it, claiming the U.S. Supreme Court had no juris-diction in the matter. At the same time, he stated that the Northwest Ordinance was no longer in effect and, thus, had no legal significance. Instead, the northern free states in question were under the legal reach of the U.S. Constitution and the state laws of Ohio and Indiana. That being the case, Taney insisted that the case was not a federal issue

The new court and its judges had no sooner met that fall than Alexander P. Field, Dred Scott's only attorney (Scott's other lawyer, David Hall, had died recently), once again filed briefs that had first been filed two years earlier. He filed both his and

---

under the Judiciary Act of 1789 and not open to review by the Supreme Court. In stating so, Taney was upholding the decision of the Kentucky court against those who aided the escaped slaves.

Even as Taney claimed the case could not be reviewed by his court because of a lack of jurisdiction, though, he still took the opportunity in his dismissal to make his position clear on cases involving "reversion." In his decision, he stated that slaves taken onto free soil and then returned to slave soil were still slaves. Their status as slaves held in Kentucky "depended altogether upon the laws of that State and could not be influenced by the laws of Ohio."* Clearly, he supported the reversion theory.

Despite Taney's "decision," *Strader v. Graham* would not have any significant bearing on the Dred Scott case in Missouri unless the state's high court decided against Scott. In their details, the cases were quite different. Scott's claim that he was free was based on having lived for years on free soil, not during a short visit, as had been the case with the Kentucky slave musicians.

When the Missouri high court did decide against Scott, *Strader v. Graham* became an important precedent for the U. S. Supreme Court. Although Taney had been able to brush *Strader v. Graham* aside because of questions of jurisdiction, he could not do so with the Dred Scott case. And Taney's position on "reversion" would prove problematic for Dred Scott's case and cause.

---

* Quoted in Paul Finkelman, *Dred Scott v. Sandford: A Brief History With Documents.* Boston: Bedford Books, 1997, p. 20.

those drawn up by opposition lawyers. He did so without even contacting Mrs. Emerson's attorneys, although they received word later. With the briefs having been presented again, the court prepared to make its decision. Judge Scott was selected to write the court's rendering, a sign that the case would not be settled in Dred Scott's favor. On March 22, 1852, Scott announced his decision on behalf of the Missouri Supreme Court, with Ryland in agreement. It was the court's ruling that Dred Scott was, indeed, not free at all, but that he was a slave and had always been a slave. This decision reversed the decision previously handed down by the lower Missouri court.

At the heart of Judge Scott's ruling was the legal issue of comity, or the "the recognition by courts of one jurisdiction of the laws and judicial decisions of another," here between national laws and policy and local or state laws. Scott spoke on behalf of state's rights over national policy-making:

> Every State has the right of determining how far, in a spirit of comity, it will respect the laws of other States. Those laws have no intrinsic right to be enforced beyond the limits of the State for which they were enacted. The respect allowed them will depend altogether on their conformity to the policy of our institutions. No State is bound to carry into effect enactments conceived in a spirit hostile to that which pervades her own laws.[49]

His point was clear: If Illinois or any other free state or territory wanted to ban slavery within its own borders, that was its choice. But Missouri, or any other slave-holding state, was not obligated to abide by those laws. To a great extent, Judge Scott based his majority opinion on one significant assumption: That Dred Scott was nothing more than property. On this point, he wrote: "On almost three sides the State of Missouri is surrounded by free soil. . . . If a master sends his slave to hunt his horses or cattle beyond the boundary, shall he thereby be liberated?"[50]

All of a sudden, with the decision of two of three state judges, Dred Scott's six-year battle to gain the freedom of his wife, daughters, and himself was ended, and all their hopes dashed. It was the 1850s, which would prove to be one of the most turbulent decades in American history. The era of Missouri Supreme Court justices who were sympathetic to slaves who filed freedom suits had ended. During that decade, the Missouri court was shifting, aligning the state more with the positions taken by southern states on slavery and any attempts to limit its regional expansion. When laying down a decision in 1852 on the Dred Scott case, the majority opinion of the Missouri Supreme Court, as written by Justices William Scott and John Ryland, signaled an end to the possibility of slaves held in Missouri suing their masters for their freedom based on residence in a free state or territory. Even cases such as *Winny v. Whitesides* were ignored as precedents. As Judge Scott wrote in his majority opinion regarding the Dred Scott: "Times are not as they were when the former decisions on this subject were made."[51]

SLAVES ONCE MORE

With their status as slaves determined, at least for the moment, by the Missouri Supreme Court, the Scotts were uncertain where to turn next. Perhaps their fate had been sealed. Their years of legal proceedings appeared at an end. Irene Emerson and John Sanford thought as much, and within weeks of the court's decision, Mrs. Emerson (now Mrs. Chaffee) contacted the St. Louis sheriff for him to forward the Scotts' wages to her. For four years, the Scotts had been hired out, and the sheriff had deposited the wages in a local bank. When Mrs. Emerson made her application to take the wages earned by the Scotts, Judge Hamilton denied her request. Hamilton also refrained from carrying out the Missouri Supreme Court's decision by not turning Dred and Harriet over to Emerson directly. The judge instead ordered the sheriff to continue holding them in custody. There is no clear reason why Hamilton would make

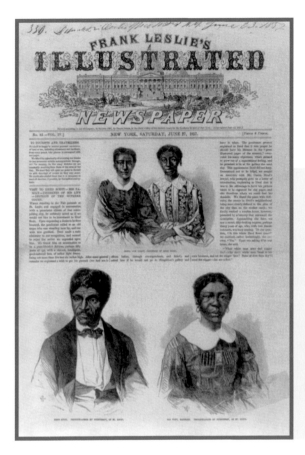

The plight of the Scott Family was featured in the June 27, 1857, issue of *Frank Leslie's Illustrated Newspaper*. Dred and Harriet Scott are pictured at the bottom of the page, while their daughters, Eliza and Lizzie, are shown above them.

these decisions, unless he had already heard from Scott's new lawyer that the case was going to be advanced to the U.S. Supreme Court.

As for Alexander Field, he would no longer represent Scott. He had moved away to Louisiana. In the meantime, Dred Scott had, during the years of his Missouri trials, been working as a custodian in several law offices. One belonged to a real estate attorney named Roswell Field (unrelated to Alexander Field), a northerner who had little sympathy for slavery. On occasion, he agreed to represent freedom cases. One of Field's associates was Edmund LaBeaume, brother-in-law to the Blow family. The Blows had remained steadfast in their continued support of Dred Scott and his attempts to gain his freedom.

When LaBeaume approached Field about the lawyer's janitor, Dred Scott, Field was interested in assisting with continuing the case.

As Field took over the Dred Scott case, he totally rethought and redirected the legal proceedings. He chose not to take the case on appeal directly to the U.S. Supreme Court, believing such a step would be pointless, since, in that era, advancing from the high Missouri court to the Supreme Court could only take place if an error had been made in the Missouri decision. With the Dred Scott case, this was no longer the situation. Instead, Field studied his options and came to believe he had found a new angle. According to Dred Scott, Mrs. Emerson had sold him to her brother, John Sanford. (LaBeaume probably told Field the same thing.) Since Sanford had subsequently moved to New York, and Dred was still living in St. Louis, Field decided that he could take a new case on Scott's behalf to U.S. Circuit Court based on his interpretation of Article 3, Section 2 of the United States Constitution, which involved cases between American citizens living in different states. Field knew what was at stake in filing this new suit: "The question is the much-vexed one of whether the removal by the master of his slave to Illinois or Wisconsin [results in] an absolute emancipation."[52] He also knew that, if the case did appear before the U.S. Supreme Court, it would be the last court the Scotts' case would ever see. If the Taney court decided against Dred, he would remain a slave forever.

To this end, Dred and Harriet Scott filed yet another suit, this time in the federal Circuit Court in St. Louis against John Sanford, whom Dred believed was his owner. The date was November 2, 1853. In the suit, Scott claimed that "Sanford had assaulted and wrongfully imprisoned [him], his wife Harriet, and their two children, Eliza and Lizzie."[53] Scott also claimed damages of $9,000 based on the three counts filed against Sanford.

The case was heard the following April. When the federal circuit court met that spring, it was not in an official court building. The court in that Missouri district had been shuffled from one rented building to another. By 1854, it was based in "a small back room over a Main Street store."[54]

The presiding federal judge was Robert W. Wells. Although he owned slaves himself, he was uncertain whether slavery could or should continue to exist much longer as strictly a southern institution. In the suit, Sanford, a New Yorker, was accused of holding Scott, a Missouri citizen, illegally. Sanford's lawyers countered that the court should not hear the case since Dred Scott was not a citizen of Missouri or of any other state in the Union. Dred was, attorneys claimed, "a negro of African descent; his ancestors were of pure African blood, and were brought into this country and sold as negro slaves."[55]

YET ANOTHER COURTROOM

Six months later, on May 15, 1854, a new Dred Scott case was presented to the Circuit Court in St. Louis. As for Dred and Harriet, it was yet another step in a prolonged series of legal attempts that had so far not brought them undisputed freedom. Their lives had been held up through these proceedings, and their future remained in question. They were still living in St. Louis in a small, temporary shelter in an alley between 10th and 11th streets in the downtown district. Harriet was hired to take in laundry, while Dred took odd jobs as he could find them. Most recently, he had hired out as a painter. Their children were still separated from them, still in safe-keeping.

Even as the Scotts received yet another day in court, national events regarding slavery and its western expansion were heating up. In Congress that spring, there was regular debate on a proposed law called the Kansas-Nebraska bill. Created by Illinois Senator Stephen Douglas, the bill sought to create two new territories from the northern lands of the old Louisiana Purchase territory. The Kansas Territory was largely equivalent to modern-day Kansas, but the proposed Nebraska Territory included today's states of Nebraska, the Dakotas, and portions of Montana, Colorado, and Wyoming. The controversial aspect of the bill was that it intended to open these new territories to the possibility of slavery being introduced there; this, despite the Missouri Compromise from more than 30 years earlier that had specifically banned slavery from these territories. The Kansas–Nebraska Bill was, therefore, a direct violation of the Missouri Compromise. Once again, just as with the Compromise of 1850, new territory might be opened to slavery. Out in Kansas, political arguments over slavery and its expansion north were causing violent encounters between anti- and pro-slavery factions.

As the case for and against Dred Scott was presented that spring in circuit court, much of the proceedings were a

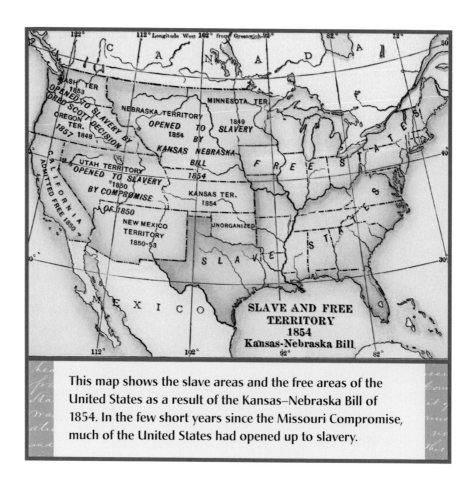

This map shows the slave areas and the free areas of the United States as a result of the Kansas–Nebraska Bill of 1854. In the few short years since the Missouri Compromise, much of the United States had opened up to slavery.

mirror image of what had taken place over the years in Missouri courts. There were no new witnesses or additional testimony or evidence presented. Scott's lawyer suggested that Dred should be freed, based on the Northwest Ordinance of 1787, the Missouri Compromise, and the laws of Illinois and the former Wisconsin Territory (which had been similar to Michigan law). The presiding judge, Robert Wells, did not agree. Instead, he sided with the Missouri Supreme Court decision. Scott had been a slave and would remain one under Missouri law, not according to the laws of Illinois. Wells did admit that Dred Scott was a citizen of the United States and of Missouri. He defined "citizen" as someone who held permanent residence in the state. The judge did not accept that Scott, even if declared free, was entitled to be treated as an equal to white citizens, however.

One of the lingering questions concerning the Dred Scott case as it appeared before the U.S. Circuit Court was that of ownership. Who actually owned Scott? Had Sanford's sister, Irene, given him ownership or had she kept the Scotts as her personal property? It is not a question easily answered. The most significant reason for assuming that Sanford had become Dred Scott's owner by 1853 was that his lawyers repeatedly stated it as fact. During the legal proceedings in Missouri, Sanford had testified that the Scott family was his "lawful property."[56] However, no bill of sale was ever produced as proof. In addition, when John Sanford died on May 5, 1857, just two months after the Taney decision was handed down, his will and the probate papers give no mention of his ownership of the Scotts. Finally, when Taylor Blow later purchased Dred Scott following Sanford's death, he bought him from the Chaffees, not the Sanford family.

Some modern historians do not believe Sanford ever actually owned the Scotts, but merely "exercised control over them in his capacity as an executor of John Emerson's will."[57] But these points beg a serious question: If John Sanford was never the actual owner of the Scotts, then why would he allow himself to be sued in the first place? Why would he not simply admit the slaves were not his?

When Judge Wells made his decision in the Dred Scott case before him, he decided against the slave. Sanford was found not guilty of assaulting Dred Scott, who would remain a slave by definition. With this decision, the earlier concept of "Once free, forever free" was no longer in place. Field had not expected to win his case, but he also wasted no time in asking for a new trial. Judge Wells denied him. The next natural step was to take Scott's case to the U.S. Supreme Court. It was not as easy a proposition as it sounded. Already the Scott trials had required significant investment on the part of the Blow family, and a national trial would be costly. To help raise funds, Charles LaBeaume wrote and sold a 12-page pamphlet telling Dred Scott's story. In the pamphlet's preface, LaBeaume wrote as if he were Dred Scott, calling on those with an interest to contribute: "I have no money to pay anybody at Washington to speak for me. My fellow-men, can any of you help me in my day of trial? Will nobody speak for me at Washington, even without hope of other reward than the blessings of a poor black man and his family?"[58]

7

The Decision

Despite the Blow family's pleas for support, almost no one stepped forward to help with Dred Scott's battle for freedom. It was a difficult time for abolitionists across the country, as the slavery issue was reaching a boiling point. In Kansas, slavery's supporters and detractors were facing down one another in conflicts that were turning bloody. The antislavery faction across the north had never latched on to Scott's cause in the courts of Missouri, and they seemed absent when Scott needed them to take his cause to the highest court in the land. Months passed and no lawyer could be found who would take on the case of Dred and Harriet Scott.

A LAWYER STEPS FORWARD

Then, on Christmas Eve 1854, a desperate Roswell Field wrote a letter to a well-known Washington lawyer named Montgomery Blair, asking him to take on Dred Scott's case. Blair proved receptive. Field had first contacted Blair months earlier and, now, perhaps hoping to tap into Blair's holiday spirit, anticipated finally convincing Blair to take the case without accepting

In the years following the Scott decision, Dred Scott's attorney Montgomery Blair served as Abraham Lincoln's postmaster general and was a target for radical Republicans.

any payment. After discussing the issue with his family, Blair did agree. He stipulated, however, that the court costs would have to be covered by someone else. Blair found that support on his own, asking Gamaliel Bailey, the editor of the antislavery publication *National Era,* to take on the project of raising money on behalf of Dred Scott's Supreme Court case. (Bailey was also known for having published the popular antislavery novel *Uncle Tom's Cabin,* written by northern abolitionist Harriet Beecher Stowe.)

Perhaps no attorney in Washington, D.C., was more respected than Montgomery Blair. He had graduated from West Point Military Academy and carried his tall, thin frame with the air of a soldier. He was a pillar in the capital's social circles, and his professional reputation was impeccable. Originally a resident of Missouri, Blair later gave that as a reason for his taking on the Scott case. Blair had practiced law in St. Louis, but left for Washington in 1853. He was especially knowledgeable concerning Missouri law, a valuable asset. Even though oratory was a needed skill for a lawyer of Blair's standing, he did not enjoy making long, windy presentations before the bar. Perhaps it was because he had a thin, high-pitched voice.

As for Sanford, he had managed to hire two extraordinary legal minds to argue his case—Henry S. Geyer and Reverdy Johnson. It had been Geyer who had replaced Missouri Senator Thomas Hart Benton in Congress. Reverdy Johnson was a former senator from Maryland and had served as attorney general under President Zachary Taylor.

On December 30, 1854, within days of Blair accepting Field's request, the Supreme Court registered the Dred Scott case. Because of a clerk's error, the case was written down as *Scott v. Sandford.* Scott's case did not make the docket of cases the Court would hear during its coming session, however. Scott and Harriet would have to wait another 14 months for their case to be heard. In the meantime, Blair sought help from other lawyers, but no one stepped forward. Perhaps the Dred Scott

Reverdy Johnson served as one of John Sanford's attorneys. A powerful legal mind, Johnson had served as U.S. attorney general to President Zachary Taylor.

case, which had remained unsung and unnoticed for nearly a decade, was becoming too controversial, too famous, and too political.

It was an election year in 1856. Politics and slavery were the issues that stirred up many Americans that year. A Democrat president, Franklin Pierce, sat in the White House; he supported slavery and believed all abolitionists to be nothing short of wild-eyed crazies. The Kansas–Nebraska Bill had been enacted, and slavery, through a political process known as "popular sovereignty," might spread into free territory, where it had been banned for decades under the old Missouri Compromise. A new political party, the Republicans, was being established, and its members were generally opposed to the expansion of slavery into the western territories. It was a volatile time for Dred Scott's case to go before the Supreme Court. The case was scheduled to be heard that February. As for the Scotts, their lives continued on as ever. They continued to work for others and receive no pay. They were still slaves, and a great uncertainty hung over them that they might never become free.

JUSTICE TANEY AND HIS COURT

The 1856 court was made up of nine justices (including Chief Justice Roger B. Taney), the largest number of justices the court had ever included. The Judiciary Act of 1789 had established the Supreme Court with only five justices, but others had been added over the years, including a sixth in 1790 and a seventh in 1807. The number had risen to nine in 1837. (During the Civil War years, the number of justices was increased to ten.)

The nine justices on the Supreme Court that would hear the Dred Scott case came from different parts of the country; four were from free states and five from slave states. Of those five, three came from families who owned slaves. Politically, they were largely Democrats (seven in all) and the others included one member of the young Republican party and one Whig. (The Whig party had largely been replaced by the Republican party, but there were still old-line Whigs around in 1856.)

Despite a nearly even split between justices hailing from the north and the south, the court was not exactly balanced on the issue of slavery. There were four northerners on the bench, but two of them generally voted against slaves in freedom cases. Seven of the court's members had been appointed by U.S. presidents who had themselves been slaveholders. The court featured only one member who was staunchly opposed to slavery, Justice John McLean. Seven justices were typically proslavery in their positions. (One of these justices, John A. Campbell, would quit the Supreme Court when the Civil War broke out in 1861 and join the Confederacy, serving as assistant secretary of war for the southern cause from 1862 to 1865.)

CHIEF JUSTICE ROGER B. TANEY

Presiding over the court when the Dred Scott case finally came before the highest court in the land was Chief Justice Roger B. Taney. Scott and other slaves similarly wanting to gain their freedom had no friend in Taney. He was a southerner, born in 1777 in Maryland to a wealthy family of slaveowning tobacco planters. As a child Taney suffered from poor eyesight and had a gaunt and thin look that he carried into adulthood. His father insisted that young Roger and his brothers gain an education and, following boarding school, Taney was tutored at home by a teacher who had attended Princeton. He went to Dickinson College, a Pennsylvania institution founded by Dr. Benjamin Rush, one of America's most famous physicians of the early nineteenth century.

After graduating as valedictorian, Taney returned to his Maryland home and soon took up the study of law. His private law teacher was Judge Jeremiah Townley Chase, who had served in the Continental Congress during the American Revolutionary War and had helped ratify the United States Constitution. After three years of study, Taney was admitted to the bar as an attorney during the summer of 1799. In time, Taney was elected to the Maryland House of Delegates. During the following years, Taney became friends with another Maryland attorney, Francis Scott Key, who would later write the national anthem, "The Star-Spangled Banner," and whose sister Taney would marry.

In 1821, at the end of Taney's term in the Maryland legislature, he moved his family to Baltimore and became one of the city's most notable attorneys. In 1827, he was appointed Maryland's attorney general. Four years later, because of his staunch

This photograph of Supreme Court Chief Justice Roger B. Taney was taken around the time of the *Scott v. Sandford* case. Although Taney once had emancipated his own slaves, he gradually drifted toward a pro-slavery stance later in his life. In an ironic twist, Taney died on the same day that his native state of Maryland abolished slavery.

support of President Andrew Jackson, Taney was appointed U.S. attorney general. Jackson later appointed Taney as his secretary of the treasury, but Taney never held the post. Congress refused to confirm Jackson's choice in Taney, since Taney had been extremely vocal in the debate over the rechartering of the

Bank of the United States. Taney had joined President Jackson in opposition to the bank, a highly controversial decision on his part.

Following Taney's failure to gain Congressional support for his appointment as treasury secretary, in 1835, Jackson appointed Taney as an associate justice of the U.S. Supreme Court. Before the Senate confirmed him, however, the court's chief justice, long-time member John Marshall, died at the age of 80. Jackson then nominated Taney to replace the deceased chief justice. Taney would be confirmed in the spring of 1836 by a vote of 29 to 15. He took his place on the bench of the Supreme Court for the first time on January 9, 1837. Taney was 59 when he was added to the Supreme Court, and he served on the high court for 28 years. By the time the Dred Scott case appeared before his court, Taney had been chief justice for 20 years. In 1856, he was 80 years old, fairly feeble, and not in good health.

SCOTT'S CASE BEFORE THE SUPREME COURT

The nine justices on the Supreme Court heard opening arguments concerning the Dred Scott case on Monday, February 11, 1856. These opening remarks took 12 hours of court time, stretched out over four days. Dred Scott's case was noted in the pages of a few newspapers, including the *Washington Evening Star* and the *National Era*, but generally it had not drummed up much interest. In the February 12 issue of the *Star*, the paper editorialized, "The public of Washington do not seem to be aware that one of the most important cases ever brought up for adjudication [judicial decision] by the Supreme Court is now being tried."[59]

The court session opened at 11 A.M., the traditional time for the Supreme Court to take up its business for the day. Generally, the court sat until 3 P.M., then the justices broke for the day. Prior to the court's opening session, Montgomery Blair had filed a written brief on the case, but there is no record of Sanford's lawyers having done the same. (As for Sanford, he had been placed in a insane asylum, having developed a mental illness.) Just before the case opened in the Taney court, Blair gained a co-counsel. Ironically, a brother to Justice Benjamin R. Curtis, George T. Curtis, agreed to join Blair as a defense counsel who was considered an expert in congressional power in the western territories.

In his presentation to the court, Blair opened by reminding the justices that it was virtually common law practice in the United States that slaves were considered free when their masters took them into a free state or free territory. He continued

THE JUSTICES OF THE TANEY COURT, CIRCA 1857

The nine justices serving on the United States Supreme Court represented a stacked deck for Dred Scott when his case appeared before them for review. Although four were northerners and five southerners, most of the court's members favored slavery and were not often sympathetic to slave freedom cases.

In 1857, the justice who had served on the Supreme Court the longest was Justice John McLean, a northerner who had been appointed by President Andrew Jackson in 1829. The second longest serving member in 1857 was James M. Wayne, who had been appointed in 1835, again by Jackson. McLean had served on the Ohio Supreme Court and as U.S. postmaster general before rising to the Supreme Court. He enjoyed politics and for decades wanted to run for U.S. president. Wayne had served as a judge in Georgia. He was a Democrat who had served in Congress. Wayne and Chief Justice Taney were the only two southerners on the high court who did not own any slaves.

John A. Campbell was the youngest member of the Supreme Court, having been appointed in 1853 by President Franklin Pierce. An by making three arguments on Dred Scott's behalf. First, Scott had, indeed, been a slave first held in a slave state, but he had been taken for a lengthy period of time into a free state. Second, by applying the concept of "once free, forever free," Scott should be considered a free man, even though he had eventually been returned to a slave state. Last, since Scott had lived in the United States all of his life, he should be considered a U.S. citizen, thereby having the right to sue in a United States court of law.

In presenting their case, Sanford's lawyers refused to accept Blair's three basic points. In fact, they attempted to resteer the case by bringing to the court a different argument against

Alabama Democrat, Campbell had served in the Alabama legislature before his appointment to the high court.

Other justices included John Catron from Virginia, who had been appointed to the U.S. Supreme Court in 1837. He was a strong advocate for states' rights, and he often voted alongside the chief justice on slave matters. Another justice was Peter V. Daniel, from Virginia. Daniel had served as lieutenant governor of his state before being chosen for the Supreme Court in 1841. He, too, was a strong states' rights advocate.

In addition to McLean, northerners on the Supreme Court included Samuel Nelson, Robert C. Grier, and Benjamin R. Curtis. Nelson, a Democrat from New York, did not enjoy controversy. Grier was a Pennsylvanian and a Democrat; he came to the court in 1846. During the Civil War, Grier remained loyal to the Union. A Harvard graduate, Benjamin R. Curtis was from Massachusetts. The court's only Whig, Curtis served on the high court until 1857, the year Dred Scott was decided. That year, he and the chief justice became involved in a serious dispute over the Dred Scott decision, which led Curtis to resign.

freeing Dred Scott. They argued that although the old Missouri Compromise had banned slavery from future, northern territories carved out of the Louisiana Territory north of Missouri, it was unconstitutional. Under that definition, Congress had not had the right or power to make decisions regarding the limiting of slavery. By invalidating the Missouri Compromise, Sanford's lawyers argued that Scott's having left Missouri for residence in Illinois did not result in his freedom. He was a slave before, he was a slave after, and, as a slave, Dred Scott had no right to sue in court to gain his freedom. Almost as soon as it opened before the Supreme Court, the Dred Scott case shifted direction away from questions regarding Scott's freedom to questions concerning Scott's right to sue at all. If he was a slave, now and forever, he had no right to sue, for he was not a U.S. citizen.

Following the presentation of the case by both sides, the Supreme Court convened for discussion on February 22. Despite involved discussions, the justices could not come to a conclusion. They recessed throughout the month of March, allowing the justices to have some time to spend on their circuits. The court then reconvened on April 5. Over the following week, the justices sat and deliberated on four different occasions.

A FAILURE TO DECIDE

In the meantime, as the justices deliberated and failed to reach a decision in the Dred Scott case, the country was continuing to witness further clashes over slavery and its expansion. Kansas Territory had fallen into a cycle of attacks and counterattacks committed by both slave supporters and abolitionists. That May, Massachusetts Senator Charles Sumner was attacked in the Senate chamber by Preston Brooks, a member of the House of Representatives, after Sumner passionately spoke out against slavery and those who support it, including Brooks's uncle, Senator Andrew Pickens Butler of South Carolina. In the attack, Brooks nearly killed Sumner by beating him with his cane.

Chief Justice Taney finally closed the Supreme Court session and held the Dred Scott case over for the court's term the following year. Once again, the future of Dred and Harriet Scott remained undecided by America's legal system.

Before the court reconvened in January 1857, though, the United States witnessed another presidential election. The newly formed Republican party nominated former Missouri Senator Thomas Hart Benton's son-in-law, John C. Fremont. The party cobbled together a strong antislavery platform that denied the extension of slavery into the western territories and confirmed the power of the Congress to limit slavery's territorial expansion. The Democrats selected James Buchanan, a northerner, as their candidate and ran a campaign in support of popular sovereignty, a political concept that allowed each territory's residents to vote slavery up or down by their choice, denying the power of the Congress to limit slavery's expansion. In November, Buchanan was elected by an extremely close vote. The Republicans had done well for themselves in their first national presidential campaign. Without courting a single southern vote, the Republicans had nearly elected Fremont.

Against this backdrop, which further fueled antagonisms between north and south, slave supporters and antislavery factions, the Supreme Court went into its new session to decide the Dred Scott case. On December 15, 1856, the justices reheard arguments from both Scott's and Sanford's lawyers. The arguments had not changed: Scott had been taken into free territory and should be considered free. The opposition argued that Scott was a black slave and did not have the right to sue in court since he was not a U.S. citizen. This latter position, if accepted by the justices, could end the trial through a "plea of abatement." Such a decision is based on a case having no legal merit requiring it be dismissed or thrown out. If Scott was not a citizen, the court could make such a decision.

As the court took up the case for a second time, the justices understood that they had several choices they could make. The question of Scott's citizenship rested in whether the Missouri Compromise was constitutional, since Scott's potential freedom hinged on the compromise being valid at the time Scott was taken into Wisconsin Territory. If the court decided that the compromise was unconstitutional, the case could be tossed out on a plea of abatement. In addition, the court could simply ignore the question of the constitutionality of the Missouri Compromise, decide that the concept of "once free, forever free" was invalid, and uphold the Missouri Supreme Court's decision made more than two years earlier.

AT LAST A DECISION

Weeks passed before the justices came to a conclusion and made a majority decision. On Friday, March 6, 1857, Chief Justice Roger Taney read the court's decision, long-awaited, especially by the Scott and Blow families. For two hours, a feeble Taney spoke. By a vote of seven to two, Dred Scott was declared to be a slave. After 11 years of legal filings, court hearings, and endless delays, the status of Scott, Harriet, and their two children remained the same, as if none of it had ever happened. The decision rendered by the Taney court was more complicated in its specifics, however. The court had gone out of its way to make additional, peripheral decisions regarding slavery, the territories, and citizenship for blacks.

Only four of the justices, including Taney, Curtis, Daniel, and Wayne, agreed that the case should have appeared before their court. On the perennial question of Scott's citizenship, three of the justices, including Taney, Daniel, and Wayne, stated that not only was Scott not a citizen, but that no blacks in America were entitled to citizenship. Thus, if Scott was not a citizen, he had never had the right to sue in court.

This point was met with strong opposition by Justices McLean and Curtis. They argued that historically, blacks had

The judgment in the U.S. Supreme Court case *Dred Scott v. John F.A. Sandford*, on March 6, 1857, stated that black people were not citizens of the United States and therefore were not entitled to protection from its courts.

participated in American politics by the time of the American Revolution and that blacks certainly had voted as citizens. Curtis, in his decision, argued:

> At the time of the ratification of the Articles of Confederation, all free native-born inhabitants of the States of New Hampshire, Massachusetts, New York, New Jersey, and North Carolina, though descended from African slaves, were not only citizens of those States, but such of them as had the other necessary qualifications possessed the franchise of electors, on equal terms with other citizens.[60]

Curtis's argument went largely unheard, however. In addition, seven of the justices (everyone except Curtis and McLean, both of whom were northerners) agreed that Scott's status would be determined by the laws of Missouri, even if he lived in a free state and territory. The concept of "once free, forever free" had been destroyed by the court.

Then, the court added to its decisions and went beyond the scope of Dred Scott and the question of his personal status and future as a slave. Two-thirds of the justices (Taney, Grier, Daniel, Campbell, Wayne, and Catron) decreed that the Missouri Compromise, which had been put into effect more than a quarter century earlier, was no longer the law of the land. The justices stated that the Missouri Compromise went against the Constitution, because its existence amounted to a violation of the Fifth Amendment, which states that a citizen may not be deprived of his or her "life, liberty, or property, without due process of law."[61]

Taney argued in his decision the logic of the majority of the court in declaring the Missouri Compromise unconstitutional:

> The powers over person and property of which we speak are not only not granted to Congress, but are in express terms denied. . . . And this prohibition is not confined to the States, but the words are general, and extend to the

whole territory over which the Constitution gives it power to legislate, including those portions of it remaining under territorial government, as well as that covered by States.[62]

The decision also answered the question of whether Congress had the power to decide where slavery could and could not exist. Taney and the majority of the court had decided the answer to that thorny issue was "No."

In deciding against the constitutionality of the longstanding compromise, it is clear why the justices decided against freeing Scott. If the Missouri Compromise was unconstitutional then Scott's claim that he should be free because he was forced to live at Fort Snelling (in Wisconsin Territory) was also invalid. According to the court, Dred Scott was nothing more than property that his owner was free to take wherever he pleased. The same, of course, would be true of all masters and slaves. Under the Supreme Court's Dred Scott decision, owners would be free, by law, to take their slaves anywhere they wished.

The Dred Scott decision of the Supreme Court soon reverberated across the United States. Although the case had gone largely unnoticed throughout the previous decade of litigation, now "Dred Scott's name was probably familiar to most Americans who followed the course of national affairs."[63] The decision exploded across newspapers throughout the country.

OF DRED SCOTT AND HARRIET

What of the man whose life and future had hung in the balance for more than a decade while the American legal system ran its full course? Put simply, the decision probably impacted him less than any other American. He had been a slave before the Supreme Court ruling, and he was a slave afterward. In 1857, Scott was still working as a custodian in the Field law offices. As for John Sanford, he likely never knew the outcome of the case that bore his misspelled name. On May 5, 1837, Sanford died in a mental institution.

It wasn't the Taney court that finally decided the future for Dred Scott, however. Within days of the Supreme Court decision, Calvin Chaffee came forward and spoke to a Massachusetts newspaper, the Springfield *Argus,* and stated that his wife was Scott's owner. Irene Chaffee (formerly Mrs. Emerson) had told her second husband that Dred Scott was still her slave—that she had never transferred ownership to her brother, John Sanford. Chaffee's public admission was an embarrassment to him. He had become a prominent Massachusetts congressman and a Republican as well, elected as an antislavery candidate.

There was little Chaffee could do but arrange for Dred Scott to be freed. He had told a newspaper in an interview that spring: "I regard Slavery as a sin against God and a crime against man."[64] He convinced Irene to agree to transfer ownership of Dred and his family to Taylor Blow. (Mrs. Chaffee could not free the Scotts herself without making a trip to Missouri.) On May 26, 1857, Dred and Harriet went to court one last time. They appeared before Judge Alexander Hamilton, who had presided over their case a decade earlier. Taylor Blow was present and signed the official and legal papers that would free the Scotts. Once the transaction was completed, in May 1857, Taylor Blow was finally able to congratulate Dred Scott, for he and his family were at last free.

In many ways, Dred and Harriet's lives remained the same following the granting of their freedom. They continued to work, but now they worked for wages. Dred took a job as a porter at the Barnum Hotel in St. Louis, at the corner of Second and Walnut Streets, and Harriet continued to work as a laundress, but with her daughters at her side. With the threat of slavery gone, the Scott family could live under the same roof once again. Dred and Harriet were offered $1,000 to tour the country and tell the dramatic story that had taken them from slavery to freedom, but they wanted none of it. They only wanted to continue working and earning an honest living.

Sadly, Dred Scott was only able to enjoy his hard-won freedom for less than a year and a half. He died on September 17,

1858, probably from a prolonged struggle with tuberculosis. He was buried in an unmarked grave in a local cemetery. By 1867, though, Taylor Blow carried out his final gesture of goodwill toward Dred Scott. He paid to have Scott's body reburied in the Blow family plot at St. Louis's Calvary Cemetery. As for Harriet, she is believed to have died in 1870. Her daughter, Eliza, had already died seven years earlier, in 1863. Lizzie Scott married and lived until 1884. In 1957, several of her descendants attended events marking the 100th anniversary of the Dred Scott decision.

Between Scott's death and his reburial, the United States had experienced its bloodiest war, as North and South separated from one another over the issue of slavery. The Civil War (1861–1865) had brought an end to slavery, and the country set out to rebuild itself, free from the stain of human bondage. The story of how America changed during those difficult decades of slaveholding would be Scott's story. His struggle had been America's struggle. It was a story told in the words that were carved upon the tombstone marking his final resting place: "Dred Scott Subject of the Decision of the Supreme Court of the United States in 1857 Which Denied Citizenship to the Negro, Voided the Missouri Compromise Act, Became One of the Events That Resulted in the Civil War." Although Dred Scott had died before the first shots of the war were fired, he had been a soldier in that war—the war for freedom for all black people held as property throughout the dark night of slavery.

Chronology

1787   The Articles of Confederation Congress passes the Northwest Ordinance, prohibiting slavery in the territories north of the Ohio River, including the future state of Illinois and modern-day Minnesota, then part of the Wisconsin Territory.

1793   Federal law requires the return of any slave who escaped into northern free states or territories.

Timeline

1795–1805
Dred Scott is born sometime during this time period, in Virginia

1832
Peter Blow dies and Dr. John Emerson completes his purchase of Dred Scott

1795

1833

1833
Emerson moves Dred Scott to Illinois

1820
Congress agrees to the Missouri Compromise

1795–1805 Dred Scott is born sometime during this time period, in Virginia.

1818 Peter Blow moves his family from Virginia to Alabama, taking the slave Dred Scott with them. That same year, Illinois is admitted to the Union as a free state.

1820 Congress agrees to the Missouri Compromise, which closes the northern portion of the old Louisiana Purchase Territory north of Missouri's southern border to slavery. Missouri is allowed to enter the Union as a slave state.

1824 Missouri Supreme Court decides *Winny v. Whitesides* in favor of freeing a slave who was taken into the free state of Illinois.

1846
The Scotts file suit in Missouri court to gain their freedom

1847
The Scotts' trial begins on June 30

1852
Missouri Supreme Court rules against Dred Scott

1857
Ownership of the Scott family granted to Taylor Blow, who frees the Scotts

1850

1858

1850
The Scotts are declared free by the St. Louis Circuit Court

1856–1857
U.S. Supreme Court hears the latest Dred Scott case

1858
Dred Scott dies of tuberculosis

1830   After moving several times within the state, the Blow family leaves Alabama and settles in St. Louis, Missouri.

1831   Dr. John Emerson makes a down payment to Peter Blow toward the purchase of Dred Scott.

1832   Peter Blow dies. Dr. Emerson completes his purchase of Dred Scott either this year or the following one.

1833   Dr. Emerson is transferred for duty to Fort Armstrong, Illinois, a free state. He moves Dred Scott to Illinois.

1836   Congress establishes the Wisconsin Territory, which includes modern-day Minnesota, where slavery is banned. By May, Dr. Emerson has been transferred to another military post, this time at Fort Snelling, in the Wisconsin Territory. He takes Dred Scott with him. That same year, a Missouri court decides *Rachel v. Walker*, granting freedom to a slave who was taken to live in a free territory.

1836–1837   Dred and Harriet Scott are married sometime between May 1836 and the fall of 1837.

1837   Dr. Emerson is transferred again, this time to a military post at Fort Jesup, Louisiana, but he leaves Dred and Harriet behind at Fort Snelling.

1838   In February, Dr. Emerson marries Irene Sanford. Emerson calls for Dred and Harriet to join him at Fort Jesup, but he is soon transferred back to Fort Snelling. Harriet gives birth to their first child, Eliza, on a Mississippi steamboat in free territory. Before year's end, Emerson is assigned to duty in Florida, but the Scotts are left in St. Louis.

1842   Dr. Emerson is finally discharged from the Army and moves to Iowa, but the Scotts still remain in St. Louis.

1843   John Emerson dies, leaving Dred and Harriet to his wife Irene and their baby daughter.

1846   The Scotts have their second child, another daughter, Lizzie, who is born in Missouri at Jefferson Barracks. Later that year, the Scotts file suit in Missouri court to gain their freedom.

1847   The Scotts' trial begins on June 30, but the case is lost on a technicality. Their lawyer calls for a new trial.

1848   The Missouri Supreme Court grants the Scotts a new trial in St. Louis Circuit Court.

1850   Congress accepts the Compromise of 1850. This allows California to enter the Union as a free state. Earlier that year, the Scotts are declared free by the St. Louis Circuit Court. In response, Mrs. Emerson's lawyers appeal the decision.

1852   In March, the Missouri Supreme Court rules against Dred Scott and designates him a slave. The decision reverses several decades of Missouri precedents that granted slaves their freedom.

1853   The Scotts' lawyers file yet another suit, this time in a federal circuit court, citing John Sanford as the defendant.

1854   The Republican Party establishes itself in Wisconsin, and Congress passes the Kansas–Nebraska Bill, allowing slavery in territories in which it had previously been banned. Dred Scott loses his case in federal circuit court and remains a slave.

1856–1857   U.S. Supreme Court hears the latest Dred Scott case and takes months to consider its decision. On March 6, 1857, Chief Justice Roger B. Taney reads the court's decision: 7 to 2 against Dred Scott, who remains a slave by law. (The previous day, defendant John Sanford dies.)

1857   Following the Supreme Court's decision, Irene Chaffee (formerly Mrs. Emerson) grants ownership of the Scott family to Taylor Blow, son of Peter Blow. By May 26, Taylor has freed the Scotts.

1858   On September 17, after less than a year and a half of freedom, Dred Scott dies of tuberculosis. He is buried in St. Louis.

1865   Congress passes the Thirteenth Amendment, abolishing slavery in the United States.

Notes

Introduction

1. Quoted in Corinne J. Naden and Rose Blue, *Dred Scott: Person or Property?* New York: Benchmark Books, 2005, p. 66.
2. Quoted in Don E. Fehrenbacher, *The Dred Scott Case: Its Significance in American Law & Politics.* New York: Oxford University Press, 1978, p. vii.

Chapter 1

3. Quoted in Winthrop D. Jordan, "Unthinking Decision: Enslavement of Negroes in America to 1700," in James Kirby Martin, *Interpreting Colonial America, Selected Readings.* New York: Dodd, Mead & Company, 1974, p. 167.
4. Quoted in Tim McNeese, *The Rise and Fall of American Slavery.* Berkeley Heights, NJ: Enslow Publishers, Inc., 2004, p. 44.
5. Quoted in Fehrenbacher, *The Dred Scott Case*, p. 15.
6. Ibid., p. 12.
7. Ibid., p. 15.
8. Quoted in Winthrop D. Jordan, *White Over Black: American Attitudes Toward the Negro, 1550–1812.* Chapel Hill: University of North Carolina, 1968, p. 134.

9. Quoted in Lisa W. Strick, "The Black Presence in the Revolution, 1770–1800" in Mildred Bain and Ervin Lewis, eds. *From Freedom to Freedom.* Milwaukee: Purnell Reference Books, 1977, p. 213.
10. Quoted in Darlene Clark Hine, William C. Hine, and Stanley Harrold, *The African-American Odyssey.* Upper Saddle River, NJ: Prentice-Hall, 2002, p. 76.
11. Quoted in Roy E. Finkenbine, *Sources of the African-American Past: Primary Sources in American History.* New York: Longman, 1997, p. 21.

Chapter 2

12. Quoted in Fehrenbacher, *The Dred Scott Case*, p. 29.
13. Quoted in Constance M. Green, *Eli Whitney and the Birth of American Technology.* New York: Little, Brown and Company, 1956, pp. 6–7.
14. Quoted in Fehrenbacher, *The Dred Scott Case*, p. 40.
15. Ibid., p. 41.
16. Ibid., pp. 50–51.
17. Quoted in Paul S. Boyer, ed. *The Oxford Companion to United States History.* New York:

Oxford University Press, 2001, p. 508.

18. Quoted in Naden and Blue, *Dred Scott*, p. 29.

Chapter 3

19. Quoted in Gwenyth Swain, *Dred and Harriet Scott: A Family's Struggle for Freedom*. St. Paul: Borealis Books, 2004, p. 6.
20. Ibid., p. 9.
21. Quoted in Fehrenbacher, *The Dred Scott Case*, p. 243.
22. Quoted in Paul Finkelman, *Dred Scott v. Sandford: A Brief History With Documents*. Boston: Bedford Books, 1997, p. 14.
23. Ibid.

Chapter 4

24. Quoted in Fehrenbacher, *The Dred Scott Case*, p. 244.
25. Quoted in Finkelman, *Dred Scott v. Sandford*, p. 15.
26. Quoted in Swain, *Dred and Harriet Scott*, p. 26.
27. Ibid., p. 27.
28. Quoted in Finkelman, *Dred Scott v. Sandford*, p. 19.
29. Quoted in Fehrenbacher, *The Dred Scott Case*, p. 248.
30. Ibid.

Chapter 5

31. Quoted in Swain, *Dred and Harriet Scott*, p. 43.
32. Quoted in Fehrenbacher, *The Dred Scott Case*, p. 250.
33. Missouri Secretary of State Robin Carnahan, "Guide to African American History." http://www.

sos.mo.gov/ archives/resources/ africanamerican/guide/ image600a.asp.

34. Quoted in Finkelman, *Dred Scott v. Sandford*, p. 20.
35. Quoted in Fehrenbacher, *The Dred Scott Case*, p. 251.
36. Ibid., p. 253.
37. Quoted in Naden and Blue, *Dred Scott*, p. 18.
38. Quoted in Swain, *Dred and Harriet Scott*, p. 51.
39. Ibid.
40. Quoted in Fehrenbacher, *The Dred Scott Case*, p. 254.
41. Ibid.
42. Ibid., p. 255.
43. Quoted in Swain, *Dred and Harriet Scott*, p. 56.
44. Quoted in Fehrenbacher, *The Dred Scott Case*, p. 257.
45. Ibid., p. 258.
46. Ibid.
47. Ibid., p. 253.

Chapter 6

48. Quoted in Fehrenbacher, *The Dred Scott Case*, p. 258.
49. Ibid., p. 264.
50. Quoted in Swain, *Dred and Harriet Scott*, p. 59.
51. Robin Carnahan, "Guide to African American History" Web site.
52. Quoted in Swain, *Dred and Harriet Scott*, p. 63.
53. Quoted in Fehrenbacher, *The Dred Scott Case*, p. 276.
54. Ibid.
55. Quoted in Naden and Blue, *Dred Scott*, p. 42.

56. Quoted in Fehrenbacher, *The Dred Scott Case*, p. 272.

57. Ibid.

58. Quoted in Naden and Blue, *Dred Scott*, p. 46.

Chapter 7

59. Quoted in Fehrenbacher, *The Dred Scott Case,* p. 288.

60. Quoted in Finkelman, *Dred Scott v. Sandford*, p. 45.

61. Quoted in Naden and Blue, *Dred Scott*, p. 83.

62. Quoted in Fehrenbacher, *The Dred Scott Case*, p. 523.

63. Ibid., p. 305.

64. Quoted in Swain, *Dred and Harriet Scott*, p. 79.

Glossary

abolition   Ending the institution of slavery.

brief   Formal outline of an argument in a legal case.

Confederacy   The 11 southern states that broke off from the United States before the Civil War.

constitutional   Supporting the U.S. Constitution.

convene   The assembling of members of a court.

corroborate   To support with evidence.

emancipate   To free someone or something, such as slaves.

faction   A party or group.

hostler   Person who cares for horses or mules.

hypochondriac   A person who suffers from imaginary symptoms and ailments.

indentured servant   A person who signs on to work for a specific time in return for travel and living expenses.

invalid   Not considered true.

legislature   A government group that makes laws.

liberty   Freedom.

litigate   To engage in a legal case.

maxim   A proverb.

orator   Speaker.

plaintiff   A person who brings about legal action.

precedent   An earlier case ruling that serves as a model for future cases.

ratify   To approve and confirm.

render   To hand down a judgement or agree on and report a verdict.

statute   A law enacted by a legislative branch of a government.

Bibliography

Boyer, Paul S., ed. *The Oxford Companion to United States History*. New York: Oxford University Press, 2001.

Dunne, Gerald T. *The Missouri Supreme Court: From Dred Scott to Nancy Cruzan*. Columbia: University of Missouri Press, 1993.

Fehrenbacher, Don E. *The Dred Scott Case: Its Significance in American Law & Politics*. New York: Oxford University Press, 1978.

Finkelman, Paul. *Dred Scott v. Sandford: A Brief History With Documents*. Boston: Bedford Books, 1997.

Finkenbine, Roy E., *Sources of the African-American Past: Primary Sources in American History*. New York: Longman, 1997.

Garraty, John A., ed. *Quarrels That Have Shaped the Constitution*. New York: Harper & Row, 1964.

Green, Constance M., *Eli Whitney and the Birth of American Technology*. New York: Little, Brown, 1956.

Hine, Darlene Clark, William C. Hine, and Stanley Harrold, *The African-American Odyssey*. Upper Saddle River, NJ: Prentice-Hall, 2002.

Jordan, Winthrop D. "Unthinking Decision: Enslavement of Negroes in America to 1700," in James Kirby Martin, *Interpreting Colonial America*, Selected Readings. New York: Dodd, Mead, 1974.

Jordan, Winthrop D. *White Over Black: American Attitudes Toward the Negro, 1550–1812*. Chapel Hill: University of North Carolina, 1968.

McNeese, Tim. *The Rise and Fall of American Slavery*. Berkeley Heights, N.J.: Enslow Publishers, Inc., 2004.

Naden, Corinne J., and Rose Blue, *Dred Scott: Person or Property?* New York: Benchmark Books, 2005.

Shifflett, Crandall. "Selected Virginia Statutes Relating to Slavery," *Virtual Jamestown*, Crandall Shifflett All Rights Reserved 1998, http://www.iath.virginia. edu/vcdh/jamestown/laws 1.html#38.

Strick, Lisa W. "The Black Presence in the Revolution, 1770–1800,"
    in Mildred Bain and Ervin Lewis, eds. *From Freedom to Freedom.*
    Milwaukee: Purnell Reference Books, 1977.
Swain, Gwenyth. *Dred and Harriet Scott: A Family's Struggle for
    Freedom.* St. Paul: Borealis Books, 2004.

Further Reading

Fleischner, Jennifer. *The Dred Scott Case: Testing the Right to Live Free.* Minneapolis: Lerner Publishing Group, 1997.

Freedman, Suzanne. *Roger Taney: The Dred Scott Legacy.* Berkeley Heights, NJ: Enslow Publishers, 1995.

Herda, D. J. *The Dred Scott Case: Slavery and Citizenship.* Berkeley Heights, NJ: Enslow Publishers, 1994.

January, Brendan. *The Dred Scott Decision.* New York: Scholastic Library Publishing, 1998.

Lukes, Bonnie L. *The Dred Scott Decision.* San Diego: Thomson Gale, 1996.

Moses, Shelia P. *I, Dred Scott: A Fictional Slave Narrative Based on the Life and Legal Precedent of Dred Scott.* New York: Margaret K. McElderry Books, 2005.

Sgroi, Peter P. *Living Constitution: Landmark Supreme Court Decision.* Parisppany, NJ: Silver-Burdett Press, 1987.

Web sites

Digital History. http://www.digitalhistory.uh.edu/supreme_court/supreme_court2.cfm.

Furman University. "Nineteenth Century Documents Project. http://alpha.furman.edu/~benson/docs/#DredScott.

Minnesota Historical Society. "Historic Fort Snelling." http://www.mnhs.org/places/sites/hfs/.

Public Broadcasting System. "Africans in America: Dred Scott Case: The Surpeme Court Decision." http://www.pbs.org/wgbh/aia/part4/4h2933.html.

National Park Service Old Courthouse. http://www.cr.nps.gov/nr/twhp/wwwlps/lessons/9stlouis/9lrnmore.htm.

Picture Credits

Index

About the Author

Tim McNeese is an associate professor of history at York College, in York, Nebraska, where he is in his fourteenth year of college instruction. Professor McNeese earned his associate of arts degree from York College, a bachelor of arts in history and political science from Harding University, and a master of arts in history from Southwest Missouri State University. A prolific author of books for elementary, middle, high school, and college readers, McNeese has published more than 80 books and educational materials over the past 20 years on everything from Mississippi steamboats to Marco Polo. His writing has earned him a citation in the library reference work, *Something About the Author*. In 2005, he published the textbook *Political Revolutions of the 18th, 19th, and 20th Centuries*. Professor McNeese served as a consulting historian for the History Channel program, "Risk Takers, History Makers: John Wesley Powell and the Grand Canyon." His wife, Beverly, is an assistant professor of English at York College, and they have two children, Noah and Summer. Readers are encouraged to contact Professor McNeese at tdmcneese@york.edu.